# Plug Your Book!

## Online Book Marketing for Authors
### Book Publicity through Social Networking

**Steve Weber**

# Plug Your Book!

## Online Book Marketing for Authors
### Book Publicity through Social Networking

**Weber Books**
**Falls Church, VA**
**www.WeberBooks.com**

By Steve Weber



Published by Stephen W. Weber
Printed in the United States of America
Weber Books www.WeberBooks.com

Author: Steve Weber
Editor: Julie Bird

13-digit ISBN: 978-0-9772406-1-6
10-digit ISBN: 0-9772406-1-4

Library of Congress Control Number: 2006909769
Cover illustration: Lauren Weber
Cover photo: Copyright 2007 JupiterImages Corp.

First Printing

# Contents


**Warning and Disclaimer**.........9

**Acknowledgments**.........10

**Foreword**.........11

**Introduction**.........15

Taking control of your book sales 15
One big caveat 16
How to use this book 16
Staying current 17

**Electric word of mouth**.........19

Riding the big river 20
Amazon's 'long tail' 20
Getting recommended 22
Personalized bookstores 23
The wisdom of crowds 24
Bubbling to the top 25
Recommendation effectiveness 26

**Amazon Bestseller Campaigns**.........31

Making the list 32
How Bestseller Campaigns work 33
... and this is success? 35
Haywired recommendations 35
Is it worth it? 37

**Amateur book reviews**.........39

Credibility through peers 40
Getting more Amazon reviews 41
Amazon Top Reviewers 42
Contacting Top Reviewers 43
Etiquette in approaching reviewers 44
Finding more Amazon reviewers 45
More ways to get reviews 46

Amazon Spotlight Reviews 46
Negative reviews 47
Countering malicious reviews 48
Old-media book reviews 49
Posting trade reviews on Amazon 51
Fee-based book reviews 51

**Building your author Web site**........................................................53
Getting involved 53
Your domain 54
Building blocks of your site 55
A survey of author Web sites 55
Your online press kit 58
Multimedia for books 59
Podcasting for publicity 61
Waiting for results 62
When to launch your site 62

**Blogging for authors**..........................................................................65
What is a blog? 66
Why blogs are better 66
Breathing the blogosphere 68
Connecting with readers 69
Blog comments: pros and cons 70
Blog style 71
Your blog's angle 71
Raw materials for posts 73
Your blog's title 73
Writing your blog posts 73
Blogging categories 75
Over the long haul 75
Selecting your blog publishing tool 77
Advertising-supported blogs 78
Blog-to-e-mail service 79

**Author blog platforms up close**.......................................................81
Business 81
Humor 82
Politics 83

Arts and crafts 83
Diaries 83
Romance 84
Memoir 84
Mystery 85
Publishing 85
Blogs into books 86

**Blog tours**..........87
Targeting host blogs 87
Google PageRank 89
Building your excerpt 90
Excerpts that sell 91
Your pitch to bloggers 92
A sample pitch 93
Your guest appearance 94
Blog conversation 95
Archiving your results 96
Encore appearances 96
More resources 96

**Social networking**..........97
MySpace: Not just for kids 98
Making friends on MySpace 100
Picking your 'Top 8' 103
Tips for working MySpace 104
Your MySpace blog 104
MySpace groups 105
Create your own group 106
Dedicated pages for titles, characters 106
MySpace books? 106
Uploading videos 107
MySpace best practices 107
Other places on MySpace 108
More social-networking sites 109

**Tag – You're it!**..........111
Personal book tagging 111
Amazon tags 112

Amazon Media Library 113
LibraryThing 114
Tag-based marketing 115
Problems with tags 116

**Advanced Amazon tools** ........................................ 119
Buy X, Get Y 119
Weaknesses of BXGY 120
Free paired placement 121
Single New Product e-mails 121
Amazon Connect 121
Listmania 123
Publicize your book 124
So You'd Like to . . . guides 125
Search Inside The Book 126
Statistically Improbable Phrases 128
Writing book reviews 129
ProductWikis 130
Customer discussions 131
BookSurge 131
Your Amazon profile 131
Amazon friends 132
Interesting people 133
Fine-tuning book recommendations 133
Pricing and discounting strategies 135

**Social search** ........................................ 137
del.icio.us 138
Smart crowds 138
Vertical search 139
Amazon Search Suggestions 140
Digg 141

**Google, Amazon, digital content** ........................................ 143
Google Book Search 143
Accidental book discovery 144
Instant Online Access 145
Ad-Supported Access 145
Google Print on Demand 146

Amazon Upgrade 147
Amazon's Mobipocket 147
Amazon digital audio 149
Amazon Pages 149

**Book promotion with e-books**..........151
Amazon Shorts 151
Client acquisition 152
Selling e-books on your site 153

**Syndicating your content**..........155
Article banks 156
How duplicate content backfires 157
Really Simple Syndication 158
BlogBurst 158
Traditional media interviews 159
Press releases 160
Protecting your content 161

**Beyond the blogosphere**..........163
BookCrossing 163
Usenet, Google groups 164
Yahoo, AOL Groups 165
Getting buzz on eBay 165

**Revenue from your Web site**..........169
Amazon Associates program 169
Barnes & Noble 170
CommissionJunction 171
eBay 171
Google AdSense, other advertising 171

**Pay per click advertising**..........173
Google AdWords 173
Yahoo Search Marketing 174

**Power tools**..........175

Amazon Sales Rank 175

TitleZ 176
Affiliate partnerships 176
Analyzing your traffic 178
Linking strategy 178
Search engine optimization 179
Keyword density 179
Length of your lease 180
Publishers Portal 181
Privacy policies 182
Web site cardinal sins 182

**Selling on Amazon, beyond**......185
Print on demand 185
Amazon Advantage 185
Amazon Marketplace 186
Catalog accuracy 187
Handling sales on your site 188
Google Checkout 188

**Other major online retailers**......191
Barnes & Noble 191
BookSense 191

**Ethics of online marketing**......195
Shill reviews 195
Spam 196

**About the Author**......197

**Recommended Reading**......198

**Index**......199

# Warning and Disclaimer

The information in this book is offered with the understanding that it does not contain legal, financial, or other professional advice. Individuals requiring such services should consult a competent professional.

The author and publisher make no representations about the suitability of the information contained in this book for any purpose. This material is provided "as is" without warranty of any kind.

Although every effort has been made to ensure the accuracy of the contents of this book, errors and omissions can occur. The publisher assumes no responsibility for any damages arising from the use of this book, or alleged to have resulted in connection with this book.

This book is not completely comprehensive. Some readers may wish to consult additional books for advice. Additional sources of information are identified in the appendices of this book.

# Acknowledgments

I sincerely thank the following people, who made enormous contributions to this book:

- **Steve O'Keefe**, president of AuthorViews Inc., who provided a careful peer review and numerous suggestions for this text. This book's section on "blog tours" relies heavily on Steve's ideas and unparalleled experience in Internet book publicity.

- **Morris Rosenthal**, publisher of Foner Books, suggested many critical improvements to this book. Morris is an innovator in niche publishing and online book promotion.

- **Jane Corn**, one of Amazon.com's top book reviewers, contributed to the sections on amateur reviews and the use of MySpace as an author platform. Jane is an expert on Internet social networking and operates the eBay bookstore "Rare and Unique."

- **Aaron Shepard** of Shepard Publications helped refine this manuscript, drawing on his unmatched experience in leveraging Amazon.com to focus attention on specialized books.

- **Christine McNeil Montano**, another Amazon Top Reviewer, provided valuable suggestions for nearly every section of this book. Christine is also an online bookseller and publishes the blog "The Thinking Mother."

- **Julie Bird**, my editor and good friend, deserves special thanks for making me look good. Even with all the expert help I had with this book, Julie still managed to find and fix several goofs before they were immortalized in print, for which I'm eternally grateful.

# Dedication

Most importantly, I thank my wife and daughter, who tolerated the many late nights and weekends I spent working on this book. Thanks also to my parents, who enabled me to grow up in a home filled with good books.

# Foreword

### *If your book is your business, this is your book.*

I have enormous sympathy for authors. Imagine spending months or years putting everything you know into a book, polishing every page to get it *just right*, and just when you thought you were finished—surprise! Now you have to learn everything you never wanted to know about book publishing and marketing.

Today it's not just self-published authors who face this daunting challenge. If you are lucky enough to land a contract with a mainstream book publisher, surprise! The marketing plan is in your mirror—go take a look. That's right, you are responsible for promoting your own book. If you don't, your publisher won't hesitate to replace you on the roster with an author who hustles.

So here you are, book in hand or about to be published, and you're presented with a task that makes writing the book look easy. Your dilemma: How can you connect your book with readers?

Fortunately, the truth is on your side. All marketing boils down to one happy conclusion: in all voluntary transactions, both sides win. I value your book more than my money; you value my money more than the book. We trade. We both walk away richer for the experience.

What that means for marketers is you don't need to con people or hard-sell them. All you have to do is show people the value, and they will gladly trade their dollars for your book.

I've been promoting books online since 1992. In that time, I have launched online campaigns for more than 1,000 books. I've worked with most of America's largest book publishers, helping many of them build online marketing departments. The book you're holding now is the new training manual.

I've worked for dozens of self-published authors, too. Faced with the enormously time-consuming process of online marketing, they usually ask me, "If this were your book, what would you do?" Now here's what I tell them:

First, read Steve Weber's *Plug Your Book!*

Second, make a copy of the table of contents.

Now, cross off each chapter as you complete the task or pass over it.

When you're finished, you've done everything that can reasonably be done to launch a book on the Internet.

If marketing is all about communicating value, what makes Steve Weber's *Plug Your Book!* so valuable? Like publishing gurus Dan Poynter, John Kremer, Judith Appelbaum, Jeff Herman, and John Huenefeld, Steve Weber drills down into the nitty-gritty with the best of them. For example, when he talks about marketing on MySpace, I tingle as he reveals exactly how to process "friend" requests.

That level of detail—such as explaining the difference between Amazon's "Best Value" and "Better Together" programs—is carried through every chapter. Weber has used most of these techniques several times and reports honestly on the results. Yes, marketing your book online is going to take time—you can't phone-in a blog tour—but following Steve Weber's map will save you time. And improve your results. And that adds up to *value* to me.

Steve Weber is hip to what is happening online today—such as social networking, amateur content, and reputation management—and he's got a keen insight into what's coming: swarms of tag clouds devouring video profiles and spitting out serendipitous links. His excitement sharing these techniques is palpable. His section on Amazon marketing programs is like an M.R.I. exam, poking into every corner of the giant retailer's vast apparatus and finding promotional opportunities at every turn, such as Omakase, Mobipocket, and ProductWiki.

Weber's honesty is also commendable, as when he warns marketers against plumping pages with phony reviews, and when he exposes the shortcomings of Search Engine Optimization (SEO).

Steve Weber's *Plug Your Book!* won't spare you the plight of all modern authors—having to get out there and push that book. But it will make your time online more productive, more pleasant, and at times fascinating as all get out!

STEVE O'KEEFE
Seattle, Washington

*O'Keefe is president of AuthorViews, Inc., a pioneer in providing online video for the book industry. An entrepreneur, writer, and university professor, O'Keefe is the author of five books, including the much-anticipated* Publicity on the Internet — Tenth Anniversary Edition *(2007). He is co-founder of the International Association of Online Communicators (IAOC) and teaches Internet Public Relations at Tulane University. Find more information about O'Keefe's projects, books, and classes at www.AuthorViews.com.*

# Foreword.1

The classic disconnect between authors and publishers is over who does marketing for books. Most authors erroneously think that once they've finished their manuscript, they're done and the book will magically sell itself. Meanwhile, publishers are convinced that they're just supplying production and distribution facilities, and their marketing program is typically, "We'll add you to our catalog."

Steve Weber's *Plug Your Book!* offers a way out of this dilemma with its practical, pragmatic and low-cost ideas for promoting the heck out of your own book, whether it's fiction, nonfiction, technical, business, or anything else.

My opinion? You'd be crazy to publish a book and not grab a copy of *Plug Your Book!* to learn the many ways that you can ensure it's a bestseller rather than a sleeper destined for the overstock or remainder shelves.

DAVE TAYLOR
Boulder, Colorado

*Taylor is author of 20 books, including* The Complete Idiot's Guide to Growing Your Business with Google. *He's an award-winning speaker, sought-after conference and workshop participant, and frequent guest on radio and podcast programs. Taylor maintains three Web logs: "The Intuitive Life Business Blog," focused on business and industry analysis, the eponymous "Ask Dave Taylor," devoted to technology and business, and "The Attachment Parenting Blog," discussing topics of interest to parents.*

# Introduction

No matter what kind of book you have, its success depends on two things: It must tell a good story, and you must find an audience for it. Easier said than done, but you might take a page from master storyteller Hans Christian Andersen.

As legend has it, schoolchildren in Andersen's 17th-century Danish town played hooky from school just to hear him spin his tales. Each time he felt like telling another one, Andersen signaled his desire by flying his kite. When the kite rose, word spread quickly, and the crowd gathered.

Can it be that simple in today's world? Can the modern author build an audience solely through community word of mouth?

Yes, you can, and you don't even need to leave your backyard. Today's authors are launching their kites to a potentially huge audience by participating in Internet communities. The big difference is, your online community isn't limited to your neighborhood—it can span the globe if you invest in some string.

More than ever, authors and readers are networking, even collaborating on books as peers. With simple Internet tools, determined writers—even beginners working on obscure projects—can find their audience. Using online communities, authors can bond with readers intimately, inspiring deep loyalty.

Internet social networking has handed authors their most powerful tool since the invention of paper. In the Networked Age, the stock of gatekeepers is going down, and the power of authors and readers is soaring.

Word of mouth is the only thing that can make a book really successful. And this has always been the challenge: How can the author break through? Until recently, it usually required "pull"—connections with powerful allies in the publishing food chain. Today, creative writers can connect with readers directly. The only requirements are a link to the Internet and the will to plug in.

## Taking control of your book sales

This year, 150,000 authors will finish their masterpiece, but most of them will be horribly disappointed with their sales—only about one-third of new titles sell more than 100 copies. Most books fail in the marketplace simply because they never had a chance: Nobody ever heard about them.

Traditional marketing and advertising is less effective than ever; people aren't paying attention to it. But *free* advertising is alive and well. The catch is, you can't manufacture free advertising; you must get it the old-fashioned way—by earning it.

Now for the first time, authors and readers can ignite word of mouth using online communities to spread the word about good books. Anyone with the skills to write an e-mail can publicize their book worldwide, effectively and economically.

Internet publicity isn't the only way to promote your book, but it's a great way to start—it can open doors you never dreamed of. The real value of online publicity is that it endures, and spawns more publicity, the kind that can't be bought. More than ever, journalists and producers of radio and television programs use the Internet to find expert commentators and new story ideas.

## One big caveat

Not every song is a hit, and not every ballplayer makes it to the Hall of Fame. Likewise, an online campaign won't make a bad book successful.

On the Internet, word of mouth is amplified and accelerated. Thanks to online communities, it's getting easier to sell good books, but it's getting harder to sell mediocre ones. Word gets around. For the strategies in this book to work, your book needs to be strong, because your best competitors are online too.

Internet word of mouth depends on an educated consumer. You're asking the reader to help promote your book, and this requires a *very good* book, according to your audience. *Bad* word of mouth will hurt your sales. Online marketing only helps a bad book fail faster.

## How to use this book

The beginning sections of this book explain the basics of online book promotion, techniques that provide the most bang for your effort. As we proceed, some of the methods will be more complicated, requiring more skill and resources. Perhaps not everything discussed here will be practical for your book.

Your job is to select which promotional techniques might work best with your audience, and then use them aggressively and tirelessly. Online publicity works particularly well with nonfiction, but can be applied to fiction too. The more techniques you try, the better your chances of success. A single strategy won't work, but a combined effort will produce results, and the effect will be cumulative.

Many author Web sites are mentioned in this book. Take time to view these sites, instead of skimming ahead. Consider what you like and don't like about what other authors have done, and apply the best ideas to your own efforts.

This book is not a quick-fix plan; there is no such thing as overnight success. It might require a year or more of steady work to see appreciable results. If that seems like a gamble and lots of work, it is. But I assure you, it's nothing compared with what it took to write your book.

Read through this entire book once. Then read it again, selecting and prioritizing what you'll tackle first. Mark on a calendar when you'll start each phase of your plan. Then get to it. Evaluate your progress after three months. Determine what's been successful, and redouble your efforts there. Then try something new.

Your freedom to use all the techniques described here might depend on how your book was published. Self-published authors who own the

ISBN and online rights for their book can promote it however they please. Trade-published authors should confer with their publisher's marketing department and get approval for their plans.

One more bit of housekeeping: Just in case anyone is curious, I have no personal connection or financial interest in any of the companies, services or persons mentioned here. There is no advertising or product placement in this book.

## Staying current

The techniques and tools of authorship and online promotion are changing at warp speed. By the time you read this book, several of the details will be out of date—Web addresses change, companies go out of business, and new tools emerge. That's why I publish a companion Web site and blog for this book:

**www.PlugYourBook.com**

There you'll find a link to Book Updates in the right column, a free reference to additions and changes that didn't make it into this book. While you're at my site, I hope you'll stay for a while to see what else is new, and post your own comments about how future editions of this book can be improved.

If you have questions about this book or anything else related to book marketing and publicity, please write to me at:

**Feedback@WeberBooks.com**

I look forward to hearing from you.

STEVE WEBER
Falls Church, Virginia

# Electric word of mouth

In 1988 a first-time author, British mountaineer Joe Simpson, wrote of his disastrous climbing accident in the Peruvian Andes. His book, *Touching the Void*, got good reviews, but wasn't too popular outside England. It sold modestly and then, like most books, began fading into obscurity.

A decade later, another climbing book was penned by Jon Krakauer, an American journalist who scaled Everest on a harrowing expedition that claimed eight lives. *Into Thin Air*, with a boost from its conglomerate publisher, was an instant No. 1 bestseller and worldwide blockbuster.

And then something really interesting happened. Bookstores started getting requests for the earlier book, *Touching the Void*. Weeks before, stores couldn't give it away, and now the book was sold out. Library copies went missing. The original hardback, if you could find one, was going for $375. Harper Paperbacks rushed a new edition onto shelves, and *Touching the Void* started outselling the new "blockbuster" by two to one.

What happened? Was it a stroke of brilliance by some publishing mogul? No, it was Joe Six-Pack, reacting to book recommendations from Amazon.com. The online store began suggesting the older book to millions of people whom it knew liked climbing books, based on their buying history. If you've shopped on Amazon, you've seen these recommendations yourself: **People who bought *this book* also bought...**

Many of the new readers liked *Touching the Void* so much, they wrote rave reviews on Amazon's site. These "amateur" book reviews, written by real climbers and armchair explorers, resonated deeply with the next wave of shoppers. More sales, more good reviews.

Ten years after the book's launch, Internet-powered word of mouth did something that no team of marketing wizards could do—it landed *Touching the Void* on the bestseller lists. The story was adapted for an acclaimed docudrama. Simpson, his writing career turbocharged, followed up with four successful adventure books, a novel, and lecture tours.

And this is only the beginning, for Simpson and all of us.

Readers are finally able to find the books they want, even in the smallest niches. Readers are finding their books at Amazon and other Web stores because they offer unmatched choice and convenience. All this is a godsend for authors, who finally have a way to build their audience effectively and inexpensively. Never has it been so practical, so straightforward, for writers to earn a living at their craft and build a following.

Today book *readers* are helping decide which books sink or swim. As an author, you can hope to be swept along with the tide. Or you can take advantage of this new environment, using the techniques described in this book.

## Riding the big river

In just a few years, Amazon has demolished the barriers to book sales. No longer are new authors summarily locked out of the bookstore. Whether your book was trade-published or self-published, Amazon will not only stock it, but *rearrange the whole store* when a likely reader arrives. And if your book sells modestly well, Amazon will do lots more—like displaying your book right inside the door, at the end of each virtual aisle, on eight different category shelves, and smack-dab in front of the cash register. Think your local bookstore might do this? Maybe if you're William Shakespeare, but the rest of us are out of luck.

Book sales over the Internet now account for 15 percent of the average publisher's business, up dramatically from 1 percent in 1997. But the real impact is far greater—it's not just the 65 million readers *buying* their books on Amazon, it's the untold millions more using Amazon's catalog and book reviews to inform their buying choices elsewhere.

Amazon is ground zero for your online campaign. It provides free worldwide exposure—exposure to *those readers most likely to buy your book*. Simply having your book properly listed for sale on Amazon can create demand for it everywhere. Whether you're a famous author or an unknown, Amazon is essential because it has a critical mass of buyers using its search engine, recommendations, and reader reviews.

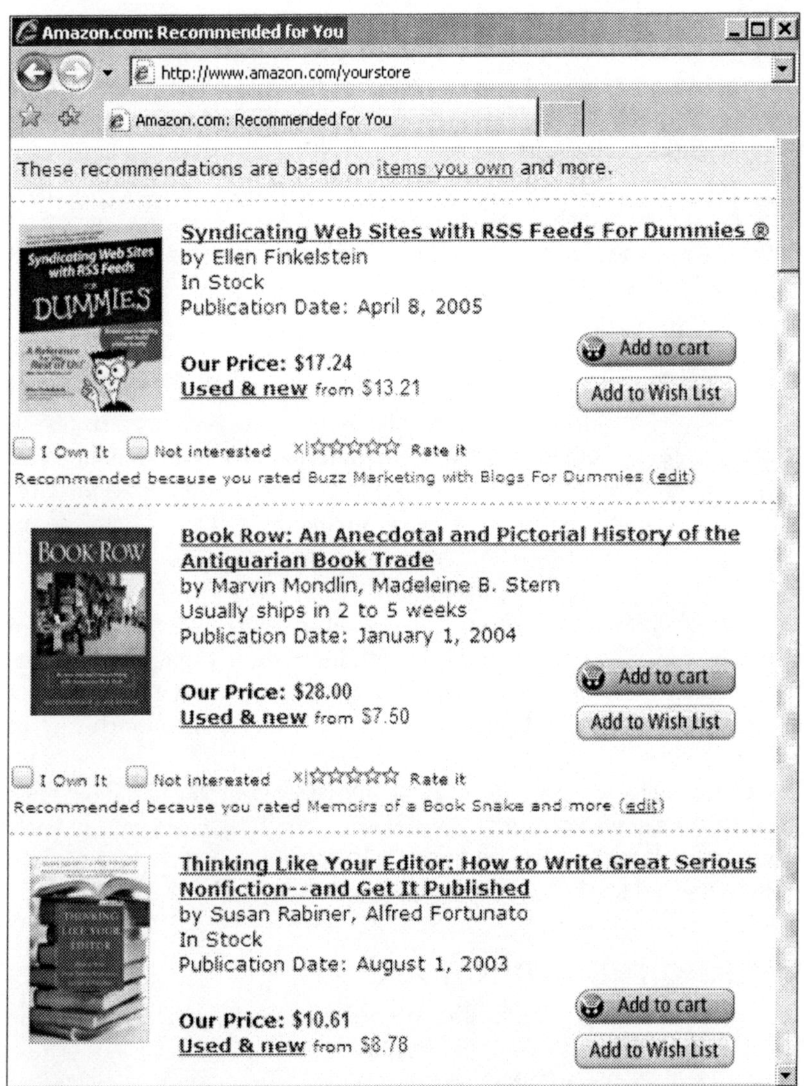


Book recommendations at **www.Amazon.com/yourstore**

## Amazon's 'long tail'

Amazon helps create demand for niche books that have a widely dispersed audience that can't be targeted effectively through traditional marketing. These are the books readers often can't find in their local bookstore, or even the library—but they're easy to find on Amazon. Twenty-five percent of Amazon's sales come from obscure books that aren't even carried in a Barnes & Noble superstore stocking 100,000 titles. And the percentage of these "long tail" sales grows every year.

Sure, part of Amazon's appeal is its discount pricing and free shipping offers. But the real value for book buyers is being able to find exactly what they want, says Chris Anderson, author of the 2006 business bestseller *The Long Tail*:

> "It's not enough that things be available, you need to be able to find them. The big problem with brick-and-mortar stores is, all shoppers experience the same store. But the problem of findability is solved when you go online. You have searching, recommendations, and all sorts of narrow taxonomies—things can be in multiple categories at the same time.

For 50 years, publishers have been chasing blockbusters—the bestseller hits. They had to, because with limited shelf space, bookstores had to focus on the stuff that moved fastest. Today, chasing blockbusters is obsolete. Authors and publishers have a wide-open opportunity in serving niches.

These niche books are the ones people care about most, and the ones Amazon is most effective in recommending, says Greg Greeley, Amazon's vice president for media products: "The Web site is designed to help customers find books they didn't know existed."

## Getting recommended

Book sales are a self-fulfilling prophecy, especially on Amazon. The more people who buy your book, the easier it becomes for the next reader to discover it. When Amazon notices your book is selling, it automatically displays your book higher in its search results and higher in its category lists. And most importantly, Amazon starts plugging your book into book recommendations on its Web site and in e-mails to customers.

Book recommendations are Amazon's biggest sales engine, after keyword searches. Sixty-six percent of sales are to returning customers, many of them acting on automated recommendations for books popular with customers with similar buying histories.

Because they are personalized, Amazon's book recommendations are network-powered word of mouth—more effective than a highway billboard seen by everyone in town. And as long as your book keeps selling, Amazon continues recommending it month after month, year after year, to its likely audience. No longer are books sentenced to the bargain bin three months after publication. Online word of mouth can keep your book alive as long as it satisfies readers.

## Personalized bookstores

Each of Amazon's 65 million customers sees a unique store. The layout is personalized, based on which books the customer previously viewed or purchased. Each customer has a recommendations list, based on which books are bought most frequently by other customers with similar buying histories.

If you have an Amazon account, view your recommendations here:

**www.Amazon.com/yourstore**

As an author, here's how Amazon recommendations work for you: Let's imagine you've written the book *How to Grow Organic Strawberries*. It turns out that one of every five Amazon customers who buys your book also purchased an earlier book, *Healthy Eating With Organic Fruit*. Realizing this, Amazon starts recommending your book to customers who bought the earlier book but haven't yet bought yours. Why? Amazon knows the odds are good that once these readers discover your book they'll buy it, too, and Amazon makes another sale.

Buyers see book recommendations in several places:

- On Amazon's home page, where it says, **Hello, [NAME], we have recommendations for you.** Click here to view all your book recommendations.

- In e-mails titled **Amazon.com Recommends** ... and **New for You**, periodically sent to Amazon customers.

- In the **Gold Box** treasure chest icon at the top right of Amazon's home page. Clicking the box reveals special offers on books and other merchandise on your recommended list.

- In a book's **Also-Bought** list. Every book's detail page on Amazon includes a list with the headline **Customers who bought this item also bought**. The Also-Bought list shows the five other books bought most frequently by customers who also purchased the displayed book.
- An extended Also-Bought list including many more titles is accessible from each book's detail page at the link Explore similar items. Buyers can view the same list during the checkout process by viewing **Customers who bought [Title] also bought...**

## The wisdom of crowds

Amazon's recommendations aren't just a computer talking, it's the collective judgment of millions of people acting independently in their own self-interest. Amazon is the biggest and most effective word-of-mouth generator for books because it measures not what people *say*, but what they *do*. People don't always recommend their favorite current book to each of their friends and acquaintances. But Amazon factors each buying decision into its recommendations for like-minded customers.

Just as a well-programmed computer can defeat a master chess player, automated recommendations can suggest just the right book, including books that would never occur to a brilliant bookstore clerk, says Amazon chief executive Jeff Bezos:

> I remember one of the first times this struck me. The main book on the page was about Zen. There were other suggestions for Zen books, but in the middle of those was a [recommended] book on "How to have a clutter-free desk."
>
> That's not something that a human editor would ever pick. But statistically, the people who were interested in the Zen books also wanted clutter-free desks. The computer is blind to the fact that these things are dissimilar in some way to humans. It looks right through that and says, "Yes, try this." And it works.[1]

---

1 Bezos was speaking at a luncheon hosted by The Technology Alliance, a Seattle-based trade group, on May 15, 2006.

## Bubbling to the top

The more your book sells on Amazon, the more frequently it's shown and recommended. Books that sell well on Amazon appear higher in search results and category lists.

Let's imagine your book *How to Grow Organic Strawberries* outsells a competing title, *Idiot's Guide to Growing Organic Strawberries*. When Amazon customers search for the keyword "strawberries," your book will appear on top—customers will see it first, and notice it before the competition.

More benefits result from your Amazon sales: Your book moves up in category lists, providing another way for potential readers to discover it. For example, your title on organic strawberries would appear in this Amazon subcategory:

**Home & Garden > Gardening & Horticulture > Techniques > Organic**

This subcategory list is like a bestseller list for your niche. Amazon has 35 top-level categories (like Arts & Photography; Business & Investing) divided into dozens more subcategories. Unlike general bestseller lists compiled by the *New York Times* or *USA Today*, Amazon's subcategory lists show what people care about at the niche level, where passions run deepest.

Amazon's subcategories are discrete enough that just a few sales can push your title near the top, exposing your book to more people who care about that topic. In our example subcategory **Home & Garden > ... Organic**, your book could claim one of the top three spots with only two or three sales per week on Amazon.

Once you've bubbled up to the top of your subcategory, you're firmly inside the positive feedback loop. Amazon acts as a huge funnel, sending thousands of readers to your book. That's why some authors encourage their Web site visitors to buy books on Amazon—each additional sale boosts their exposure, prompting yet more sales.

"Simply put, the more customers you send to Amazon who buy your book, the more visible it will be on Amazon, and the more books Amazon will sell for you," says Morris Rosenthal, publisher of Foner Books.

If your book continues selling for six months or so, Amazon can assign it to more categories, making it even more likely browsers will find you after browsing in related categories. Books that sell moderately well eventually can be assigned to 12 or more categories, the same exposure as your book being shelved in a dozen different sections of a brick-and-mortar bookstore. The big difference is, Amazon is the world's largest bookstore.

To see your book's subcategory assignments on Amazon, find the section on your book's detail page headed **Look for similar items by category**. Clicking on those links takes you to a list of the subcategory's bestsellers.

Sometimes persistent publishers can talk the folks at Amazon into assigning their books to additional categories, or removing the book from inappropriate categories. Research other books in your niche, and see which categories they're displayed in.

Narrow a list down to 10 categories and send your list, ISBN, and contact information to Amazon. You can send your message, along with any other typographical corrections for Amazon, by using this form:

**www.Amazon.com/gp/help/contact-us/typographical-errors.html**

## Recommendation effectiveness

Online recommendations are more effective with certain categories of books and price points, according to a 2006 study, *The Dynamics of Viral Marketing*. Researchers at HP Labs and two universities reviewed millions of book purchases resulting from online recommendations.

Recommendations for medical texts tended to be most effective—nearly 5.7 percent of them resulted in a purchase, almost double the average rate. The researchers attributed this to the higher median price of medical books and technical books in general. A higher book price increased the chance that recommendations would be consulted and accepted.

Recommendations were moderately effective for certain religious categories: 4.3 percent for Christian living and theology, and 4.8 percent for Bibles. By contrast, books not connected with organized religions had lower recommendation effectiveness, including New Age (2.5 percent) and occult (2.2 percent).

Recommendations for fiction books were usually the least effective, with only about 2 percent resulting in purchases. Recommendations for nonfiction books dealing with personal and leisure pursuits were slightly more effective, resulting in purchases about 3 percent of the time.

**Figure 1.1**

## Recommendation effectiveness by category

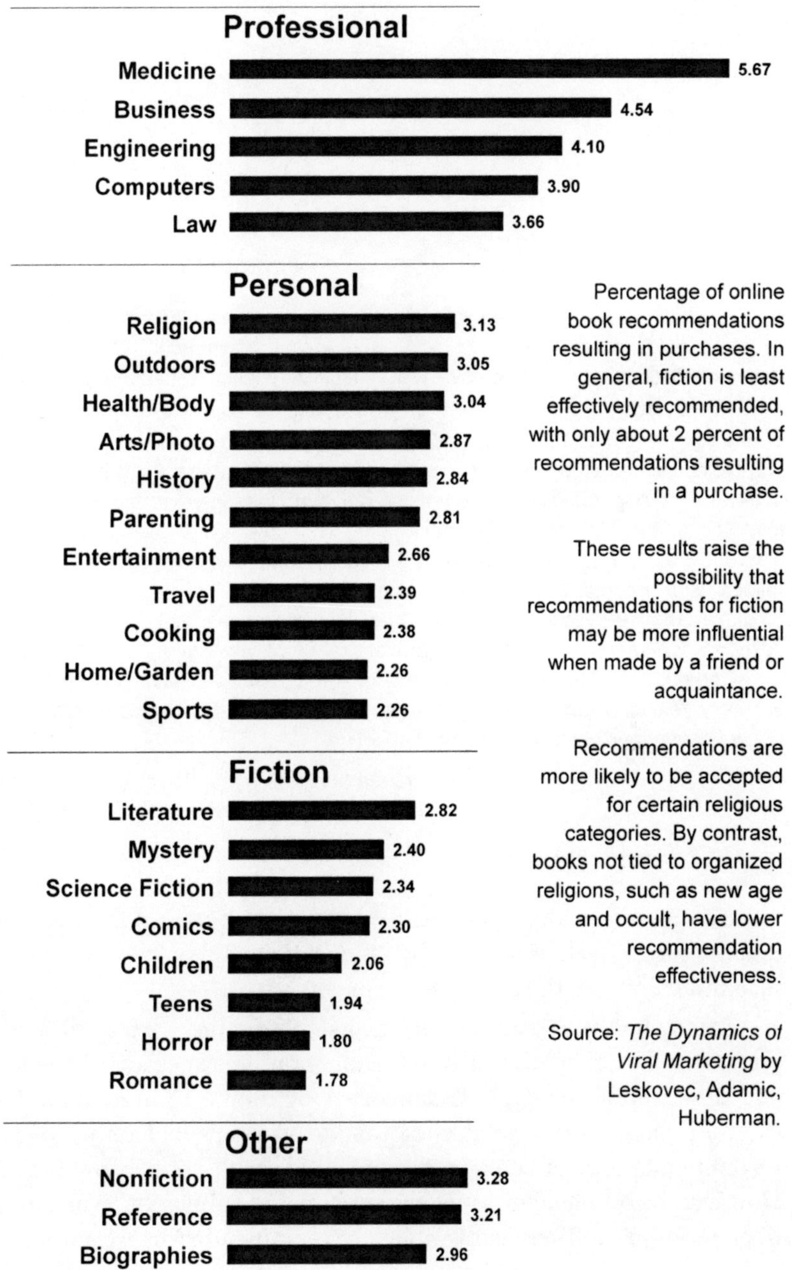


Percentage of online book recommendations resulting in purchases. In general, fiction is least effectively recommended, with only about 2 percent of recommendations resulting in a purchase.

These results raise the possibility that recommendations for fiction may be more influential when made by a friend or acquaintance.

Recommendations are more likely to be accepted for certain religious categories. By contrast, books not tied to organized religions, such as new age and occult, have lower recommendation effectiveness.

Source: *The Dynamics of Viral Marketing* by Leskovec, Adamic, Huberman.

**Figure 1.2**

## Extremes in book recommendation networks

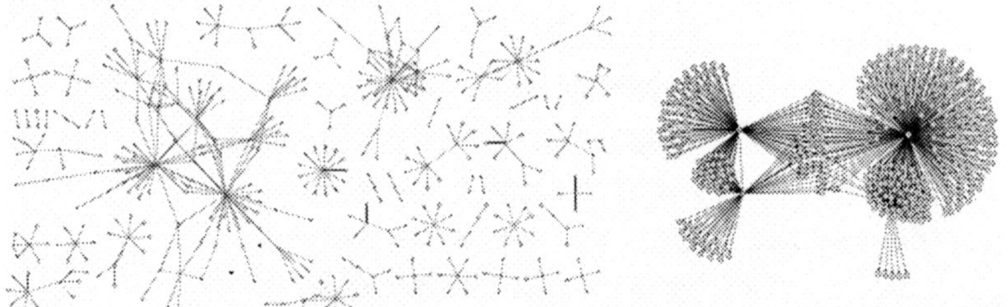

**study guide** **Japanese graphic novel**

Two book recommendation networks. The left shows how recommendations for a study guide were ineffective and ignored by consumers. On the right, recommendations for a graphic novel were effective, resulting in frequent purchases.

The book on the left is the study guide *First Aid for the USMLE Step 1.* The book on the right is *Oh My Goddess!: Mara Strikes Back.* Recommendations for this graphic novel prompted bursts of connected sales represented visually by the linked patterns. The opportunities for networking are vast: Japanese comics have a wide following in the United States, are popular with children and adults, and are vigorously supported by online communities. By contrast, suggestions for study guides usually come outside online communities, originating with an instructor or employer. Choice is restricted, online connections are sparse, and no word of mouth occurs. For a variety of reasons, readers are rarely passionate about textbooks.

Generally, though, fiction recommendations are least effective of any book category, resulting in purchases only 2 percent of the time, while recommendations for expensive medical books are most effective.

*Illustration from* The Dynamics of Viral Marketing
*by Leskovec, Adamic, Huberman.*

---

Recommendations from family members or personal friends were much more effective for fiction and religious books than online recommendations, the researchers concluded.

Some book categories, such as gardening, have different recommendation effectiveness depending on how specialized the text and how widely the topic is supported by online communities. For example, books on vegetable or tomato growing had only average recommendation effectiveness compared with other nonfiction. However, recommendations of books on orchid cultivation, which tend to be more specialized, had double the recommendation acceptance.

Customers are more likely to buy a book if they receive the same recommendation twice. After that, customers tend to ignore the recommendation.

The study is available in its entirety here:

**www.hpl.hp.com/research/idl/papers/viral/viral.pdf**

## Amazon Sales Rank

As your sales on Amazon increase, you'll see a corresponding move in your title's Amazon Sales Rank.

Amazon's rankings show how each book is selling compared to every other title in the catalog of nearly 4 million. Updated hourly, the system assigns a unique rank to each book relative to each other title's sales—the top-selling book is ranked 1, and the slowest-selling book is ranked over 3,500,000.

The closer you get to 1, the more often your book appears in Amazon recommendations. For this reason, many entrepreneurial authors and publishers concentrate on driving as many sales as possible to Amazon during a book's launch. Enlarging your book's footprint on Amazon can pay dividends for years to come.

Your book's Amazon Sales Rank is public evidence of how successful your book is. Many booksellers, publishers, and agents pay close attention to Amazon ranks. So if you manage to pump up the sales rank of your book, it can prompt brick-and-mortar stores to order more copies. Publishers looking for a complementary title might ask you to write the book for them.

# Amazon Bestseller Campaigns

The Internet has become an effective marketing tool for authors because it enables your audience members to find *you*, instead of you finding *them*. With online word of mouth, you gently reel your audience in, instead of blasting an advertisement to a crowd that isn't listening.

Let's face it, traditional advertising is dying, and it never worked with books anyway. More than ever, people are tuning out commercials, junk mail and spam.

There is no shortcut for getting word of mouth for your book. And as we'll see, not only are shortcuts ineffective, they can backfire.

One shortcut many new authors are trying these days is "Amazon Bestseller Campaigns." And who can blame them: What author doesn't want to have a No. 1 book and millions of loyal readers?

Amazon doesn't endorse these campaigns, but doesn't really discourage them either. Independent marketing consultants charge $2,700 for their Bestseller Campaign courses, and to a new author it might seem worth every penny. According to advertisements by these Bestseller consultants, one author racked up more than $35,000 in book sales during the first 48 hours of her campaign. Could it happen to you? You bet—you'll have a "guaranteed" bestseller within "38 days."

So go ahead, dream a little. Once your book tops the chart at Amazon, you'll be on the red carpet. Lunch with publishers. Bookstore tours. Agents calling. Movie deals, foreign rights sales. And next, you'll be on the *real* bestseller lists: *New York Times*, *USA Today*, and *Wall Street Journal*.

So what's wrong with all that? The bestseller consultants say they're simply applying good old-fashioned marketing to the digital age. But critics say these campaigns are just smoke and mirrors. These consultants don't discuss whether the book needs to be any good. Apparently anyone who coughs up $2,700 is guaranteed a bestseller.

Is it too good to be true? Are these programs worth it, or just a waste of time and money?

Let's boil it down to three essential questions:

1. Are Amazon Bestseller Campaigns profitable? Do they generate more income for the author or publisher than they cost?
2. Do these campaigns enhance the reputation of the author and the book?
3. Most importantly, does the bestseller promotion provide enduring word of mouth for the book, or do sales evaporate quickly?

## Making the list

We're list-crazy these days. Everything is ranked: books, movies, radio and TV shows, Web sites, video games. The lists are dutifully reported in newspapers, magazines, and even mentioned on news broadcasts. Who's No. 1 today? Who's up and who's down? How many gazillion dollars did the latest Hollywood blockbuster rake in last weekend?

Actually, this stuff matters a lot: Most of your sales happen *after* you're on a list, because that's how lots of people discover you. For years, big publishers have used every trick in the book to break onto lists like the New York Times Best Sellers. One way is to offer huge discounts to certain retailers who place big orders, making demand appear strong.

For struggling authors, Amazon is the most democratic list because *everyone* gets on it, whether they sell tons of books or just a few. Each author who has sold at least one copy of his or her book on Amazon is ranked somewhere in

> It's easy to check the Amazon Sales Rank of any book. Scroll down the book's product page to the section labeled **Product Details**. The Sales Rank is at the bottom of the section.
>
> **Product Details**
> **Paperback**
> **Publisher:** McBride Pub; 6th edi n (January 1
> **ISBN:** 0930313062
> **Shipping Information:** View s ng rates ar
> **Average Customer Review:** based on
> **Amazon.com Sales Rank:** #49,486 in Books

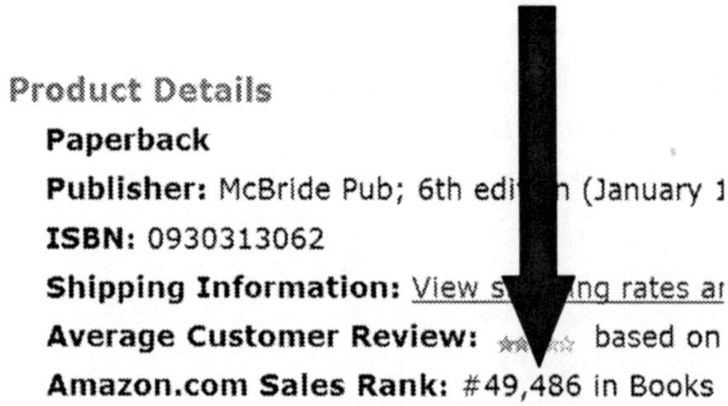

the 4-million-title catalog. The top dog has an Amazon Sales Rank of 1, and is racking up thousands of sales a day. The worst laggard is ranked 3,500,000-plus, selling perhaps one copy every few years.

Just for kicks, plenty of authors buy a copy or two of their book on Amazon, just to watch their Sales Rank spike a few thousand notches higher toward No. 1. But your Sales Rank slides right back down unless someone else buys another copy pretty soon.

Whether an author is No. 5 or No. 539,000, many simply can't resist checking their rank several times a day. And since Amazon's bestseller list is recalculated hourly based on the preceding hour's sales, the list changes 24 times a day. It's so dynamic, a short burst of sales can shoot a book toward the top. And that's what makes it fairly easy to create a bestseller on Amazon—or *rig* one, depending on your point of view.

True, Amazon is the world's biggest bookstore. But you'd need tons more sales to make the *New York Times* list, which is based on weekly sales from 4,000 bookstores and wholesalers serving another 60,000 retailers. With an Amazon Bestseller Campaign, however, you might simply line up 250 people to buy your book at 3 a.m. next Sunday, and you're No. 1. Sure, it's only for an hour, but you can put "bestselling author" on your resume for the rest of your life, right?

Well, let's get real. "Ranking high on Amazon certainly feels good, but it doesn't take many sales to achieve that," said Jacqueline Deval, publisher of Hearst Books and author of *Publicize Your Book.*

The problem is, Bestseller Campaigns are a seductive "quick fix" for authors who feel they don't have the time, energy, or know-how for real grass-roots marketing. It's frustrating to pour your heart and soul into a book for months or years, and then nobody buys it. Amazon Bestseller Campaigns can sound like a good solution, simply because they promise instant success.

## How Bestseller Campaigns work

The core of an Amazon Bestseller Campaign is an e-mail advertisement blasted to thousands of people; some practitioners say it requires at least 300,000 messages to make any difference at all. People who get the e-mails are offered a one-time deal: a long list of "valuable free bonuses" like e-books, audio files of seminars, and other digital goodies, but only if they buy your book at Amazon on the day of your campaign.

**Figure 2.1**

# Books pushed with 'Bestseller' Campaigns

These books are touted as "Amazon Bestseller" success stories by the marketing consultants who helped launch the books. However, this look at their Amazon Sales Ranks reveals poor sales that became even weaker and more erratic over time. Peaks on the chart show periods of weak sales, valleys represent strong sales. **Conclusion: Sales can deteriorate badly for books marketed with special gimmicks.**

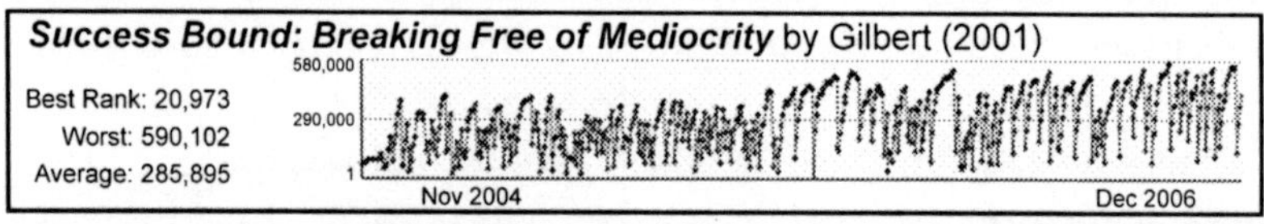


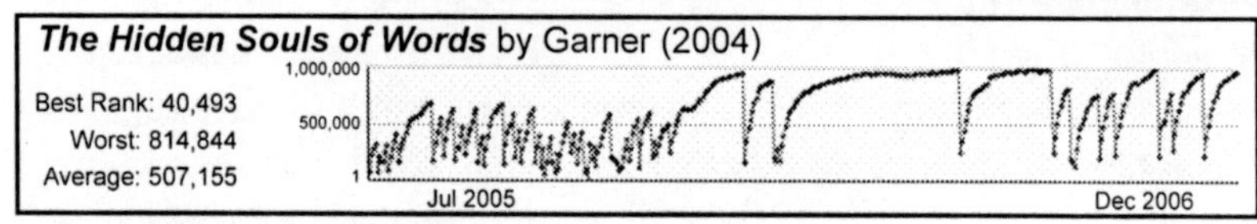

# Books plugged with online word of mouth

Word of mouth for these four books was established by the authors, using a Web site or blog. Notice the long-term trend is flat, indicating steady sales. **Conclusion: Books with Internet word of mouth can sell strongly year after year.**

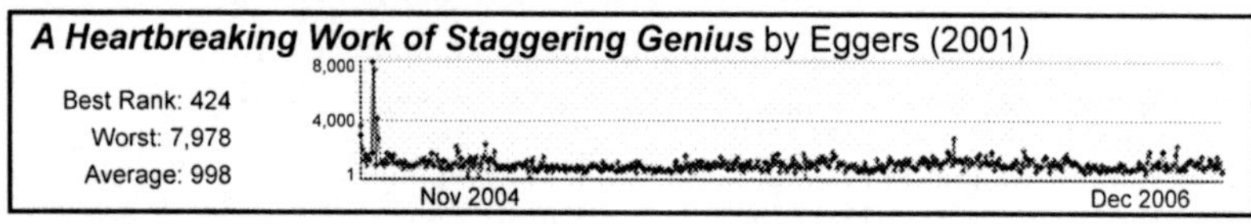


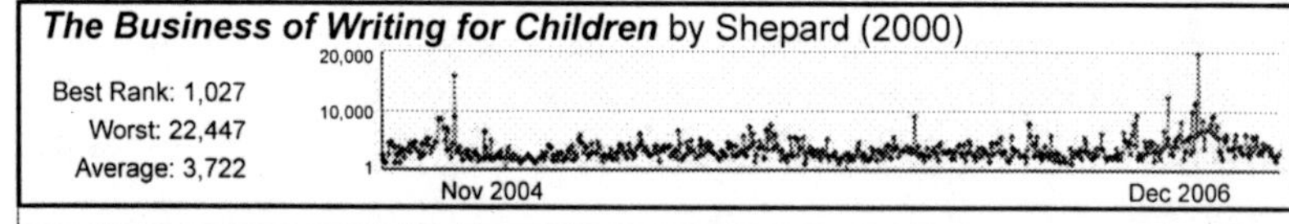


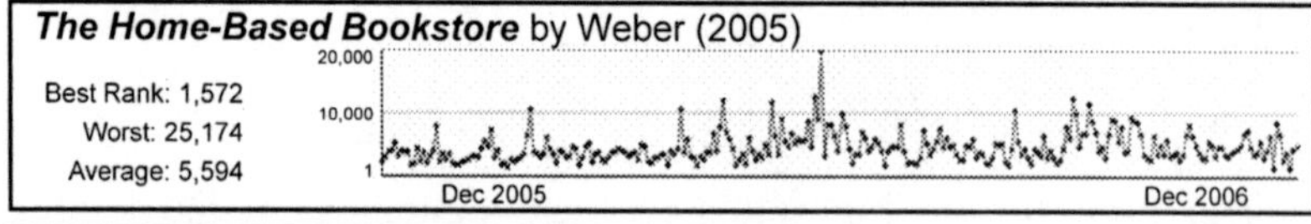


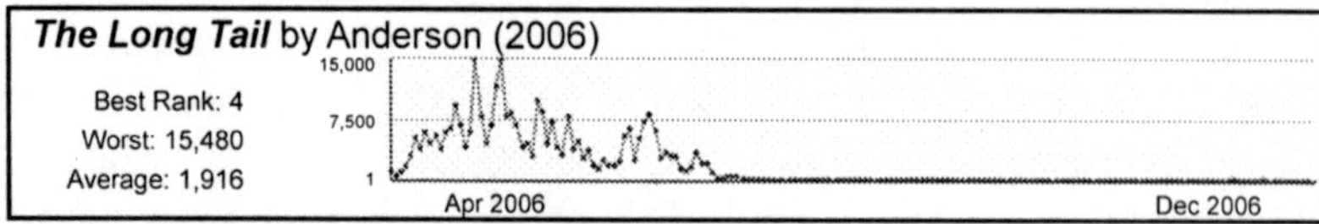


*Charts provided by TitleZ.com, reprinted with permission. In some cases, charts don't extend all the way to back to the date of publication, when sales might have been strongest.*

With some Bestseller Campaigns, buyers are offered many more freebies if they buy two, three, or even 20 copies of your book at the same time. The bonuses are advertised as being worth hundreds or even thousands of dollars.

The e-mail blasts are sent to registered subscribers of e-mail newsletters, so the messages aren't illegal spam. But just in case things don't go as well as planned, some consultants suggest you also pester your family, friends, and coworkers to buy your book on the special day to ensure it has enough sales to move up.

## ... and this is success?

The marketing literature for Bestseller Campaigns give plenty of references that seem to back up the promises. Dozens of earlier Bestseller Campaign books are listed as success stories. But a quick check of their actual sales on Amazon reveals that several of these books haven't been successful at all.

As shown in Figure 2.1, the sales charts for these books zigzag all over the place, a sure sign the book is going nowhere. Further, look at the sales ranks—they're a long, long way from No. 1. Obviously, these books are selling only a few copies a year on Amazon.

And these are the success stories? The flameouts must be spectacular.

On the other hand, look at the three bottom sales charts in Figure 2.1, the ones for books promoted with Web sites and blogs. Their sales ranks are much stronger, and the trend lines are flat, meaning steady sales. These books probably sell more copies each day on Amazon than the "Bestsellers" rack up in a whole year.

## Haywired recommendations

What goes wrong with the Bestseller Campaign books? Some of them are probably wonderful books, but nobody's buying. Meanwhile, books with genuine word of mouth can have strong, steady sales for years.

A bit more digging into these Bestseller Campaigns shows the real reason they can collapse. When readers follow their own curiosity, they tend to buy lots of the same kinds of books. For example, the Amazon customer who buys *Andrew Jackson: His Life and Times* tends to buy the following books, in precisely this order:

*Team of Rivals: The Political Genius of Abraham Lincoln*
*The Rise of American Democracy: Jefferson to Lincoln*
*1776*
*His Excellency: George Washington*
*The River of Doubt: Theodore Roosevelt's Darkest Journey*

Easy to see the connection, isn't it? These five titles are the Also-Bought list, the guts of Amazon's recommendation engine. (You can see the Also-Bought list for any book on Amazon under the heading **Customers who bought this item also bought**....") Customers who've bought only some of the books on the list soon receive recommendations for the rest in personalized e-mails or on the Web site. This results in tons of sales, and Amazon has it down to a science.

Bestseller Campaigns, however, throw a monkey wrench into this recommendation process. Instead of Amazon recommending similar books, it spits out unrelated books. For example, one Bestseller Campaign book, *Hidden Souls of Words*, is categorized Religion/Spirituality but its Also-Bought list includes completely different kinds of books:

*The Attractor Factor: 5 Easy Steps for Creating Wealth...*
*How to Be Wildly Wealthy FAST: A Step-by-Step Guide...*
*Turning Passions into Profits: Three Steps to Wealth and Power*
*The Biology of Belief: Unleashing the Power of Consciousness...*
*Life's Missing Instruction Manual: The Guidebook You Should...*

What's the connection? There isn't any, except they're all Bestseller Campaign books. They were all pitched, high-pressure, perhaps to the same lists of people, no matter what their tastes in books. A few people bought, but some of them may have wanted the "valuable free bonuses," not the book.

And now we see the real problem: Amazon isn't recommending *Hidden Souls of Words* to anyone who actually might want to read it—

people who like Religion/Spirituality books. This book's best chance at word of mouth is gone.

To be fair, a few of the Bestseller Campaign success stories really are bona-fide successes, including books by Gary Renard, Gary Rebstock, Dr. Bruce Lipton and Joe Vitale. Books by these authors sell year after year on Amazon, but is it because somebody ran an Amazon Bestseller Campaign? Or is it because these authors energetically promote their books year after year by blogging, writing articles, and giving interviews?

To be doubly fair, the consultants who advertise Amazon Bestseller Campaigns would surely tell you that a single technique doesn't support a book for long; steady sales depend on continuous promotion. Still, the question remains: Why do their clients actually fare so poorly?

Authors who ignite real word of mouth using techniques described in this book can draw a real audience who buys and recommends their book. But don't expect to hit the jackpot next month, if ever. Nothing in publishing is simple, easy and guaranteed.

Another problem with Bestseller Campaigns is the increasing unreliability of e-mail blasts. Despite laws against spam, junk e-mails are a growing problem. Increasingly, Internet Service Providers are deleting some e-mail blasts, even legitimate ones.

## Is it worth it?

It's pretty easy to do the math on Bestseller Campaigns. If you assume a cost of $2,700 and a profit on each book of $5, you'll need to sell 450 books to break even. (That's if you do the campaign yourself after taking the classes; if the consultant does it for you, it costs $15,000.)

The bigger question is, could your time and money be better spent sparking real word of mouth for your book?

If it's important to have a stellar Amazon Sales Rank for a day, you can do it much faster and cheaper by simply buying a few hundred copies of your book from Amazon yourself. Have a copy shipped to each member of your high-school class, your neighbors and in-laws, and every newspaper and magazine editor in your region. That would spark some *real* word of mouth for your book.

Beating people over the head isn't going to create demand for your book. Instead, create a way for readers to find you on their own. *That's* when you'll have an audience, and that's what this book is all about.

# Amateur book reviews

Keith Donohue had an idea for a book, a story rattling around in his brain for years. But he could never find the time to write it. With a full-time job and a family with three young children, putting it off was easy.

Then Donohue turned 40, and a short time later came the events of Sept. 11, 2001. He decided, "It's now or never," and the red-haired Irishman began writing. He wrote on scraps of paper on the subway to work in Washington, D.C., and scribbled during his lunch hour sitting on park benches.

Finally, after several months of rewriting and polishing, the story was finished: *The Stolen Child*, a fantasy inspired by the W.B. Yeats poem and what Donohue knew of the changeling legend.

And that's when things got really hard. It took Donohue two years to find an agent to shop the manuscript to publishers, nearly causing him to give up. He received 10 rejections, and was considering self-publishing. Then Donohue got a call from an agent who'd had the manuscript for a year but misplaced it. Soon, publisher Nan Talese, who runs an imprint at Doubleday, took on the book, and it seemed success was at hand.

At last, Donohue's book was in print. But then another hurdle, seemingly worst of all: The critics weren't impressed with *Stolen Child*. In fact, they completely ignored it; not a single major newspaper reviewed it. Ask any big publisher, and they'll tell you: Any novel stiffed by the critics has no chance of becoming a bestseller.

But the story wasn't over. A review copy of the book ended up in the hands of Linda Porco, Amazon.com's merchandising director. She passed it among her office mates, and it was unanimous—everyone loved it. So Porco tried something new. She got more copies of the book and mailed them to Amazon's most active customer reviewers. They review books on the site as a hobby, assigning five stars to the books they love, one star to the books they hate, and an essay explaining why.

Within weeks, all but one of those Amazon Top Reviewers posted a rave review. Promptly, *Stolen Child* became Amazon's bestselling fiction book, and reached No. 26 on the New York Times extended bestseller list, an unbelievable climb for a novel with no big newspaper or trade reviews. Now the book is in its eighth printing and the story is being shopped to Hollywood. And—oh yeah—now *Stolen Child* has plenty of professional reviews.

All this caused quite a stir in publishing circles, but it didn't surprise the folks who actually buy books. Increasingly, readers turn to online reviews written by peers to find out if a book is worth it. Talese, the publisher, says a traditional function of professional critics—building awareness of a new book—is practically obsolete in the Internet age:

> We're really trying to reach readers. Critics have been a way of announcing that a book exists that readers might be interested in. But [reviews] are being given less and less room in the newspapers.

Critics argue that amateur reviews are meaningless, that they don't apply the professional critics' intellectual rigor. But when was the last time you ran out and bought a book after seeing it reviewed in a newspaper or magazine? The truth is, many "professional" reviews are simply rehashes of publisher-generated publicity. Most of the time, professional critics don't tell readers the one thing they want to know—whether they'll like the book. Today, all it takes is a quick skim of customer reviews on Amazon, and you've got your answer. Whatever the amateur reviewers lack in highbrow sensibilities, they make up in credibility and relevancy.

## Credibility through peers

Successful books have lots of positive reviews on Amazon, and it's no coincidence. It's another point in the positive feedback loop: Good books garner good reviews, which leads to more sales. Good reviews on Amazon are particularly crucial for books by new authors and niche books.

Positive reviews on Amazon boost your sales not only on Amazon, but everywhere people are buying books. What percentage of buyers at brick-and-mortar bookstores actually made their choice by reading Amazon customer reviews? There's no way of knowing exactly, but rest assured it's a substantial and growing number.

Amazon's reviews are effective because they're often written by people who are knowledgeable and passionate about the book and its topic. They're seen as an objective evaluation from someone with no ax to grind. Sure, many inept and biased reviews appear, but they're easily ignored and far outweighed by the good ones.

In the case of a niche book, an amateur reviewer with the right expertise in the topic can critique it better than any professional reviewer can.

## Getting more Amazon reviews

Traditional book marketing strategies call for mailing hundreds of review copies to reviewers at magazines and newspapers. But for a new author with a niche book, chasing print reviews can be more of a distraction than a strategy. A better way to launch your campaign is by finding 100 to 300 readers in your target audience and *giving them your book*. Ask them to post an honest critique on Amazon. This costs nothing more than mailing review copies to traditional book reviewers, but will likely have a bigger, more immediate impact. Here's where to find review candidates:

- From Amazon's list of Top Reviewers who regularly post reviews of books similar to yours.
- Amazon users who have reviewed related titles, or books by authors with a writing style similar to yours.
- Acquaintances and colleagues interested in your book's topic.
- Participants in Internet discussion boards and mailing lists relevant to your book.
- Registered visitors of your Web site or readers of your blog.

You can find more prospective reviewers by posting a message on Amazon's discussion board dedicated to customer book reviews:

**http://forums.prosperotechnologies.com/n/mb/listsf.asp?webtag=am-custreview**

Will giving away several dozen copies of your book hurt its sales? Perhaps you'll lose a sale or two, but you'll gain much more from word of mouth. The initial readers who enjoy your book will recommend it to friends, and those new readers will recommend it to more.

Don't ask for reviews from people who haven't actually read your book, even your mother. The result will be an unconvincing review that will detract from your book's credibility rather than bolster it.

## Amazon Top Reviewers

*Stolen Child* author Keith Donohue was lucky that Amazon Top Reviewers helped make his book a bestseller; it wasn't part of his plan. But you don't need to depend on luck. Seek out Top Reviewers yourself and ask them to read and review your book. This takes some legwork, but if your book is a good one, it will be well worth the trouble. Reviews from some of Amazon's Top Reviewers can seriously boost the credibility of your book.

Amazon's Top Reviewers are listed here:

**www.amazon.com/gp/customer-reviews/top-reviewers.html**

Top Reviewers have a special badge accompanying their pen names, such as *Top 1000 Reviewer, Top 500 Reviewer, Top 50 Reviewer, Top 10 Reviewer* or *#1 Reviewer*. Having one of these badges displayed among your book's reviews isn't the same thing as an endorsement by Amazon—it's better. It's a vote by a recognized community leader—someone who takes reviewing seriously, and has earned a reputation for helpfulness.

Rankings of the Top Reviewers are determined by a point system based on the number of reviews written and the number of positive votes those reviews receive when people click **Yes** in response to "Was this review helpful to you?"

Top Reviewers are regular Amazon customers who simply enjoy reading and critiquing lots of books. Many of them review several books per week—sometimes at the invitation of an author or publisher, but usually by just following their personal interests. Despite receiving no payment for their efforts, Amazon Top Reviewers compete furiously to climb the rankings ladder. The No. 1 reviewer, Harriet Klausner, has posted more than 12,000 reviews and, not surprisingly, says she's a speed-reader. It's not unusual for Klausner to post 10 or more reviews in a single day.

## Contacting Top Reviewers

Clicking on a reviewer's pen name takes you to their Amazon profile containing biographical and other information they've posted about themselves. Some reviewer profiles will explain what types of books they prefer. For example, some reviewers stick with fiction; some review only movies or music. Some profiles indicate whether the reviewer accepts unsolicited books, and some provide a postal or e-mail address.

But Amazon gives you a way to reach reviewers who don't display any contact information on their profiles. At the top right of the profile page, click the link Invite to be an Amazon Friend. This generates a pop-up form where you can enter a message, and Amazon will forward it in an e-mail. This maintains the reviewer's privacy, and if they aren't interested, they may simply ignore your message.

A soft-sell approach works best when approaching Top Reviewers. Offer a complimentary book in return for their *considering* to review it, no obligation. Most Top Reviewers don't want to commit to a review until they've seen the book. Don't ask reviewers to return the book.

Here's a sample script you might use to approach Amazon Top Reviewers:

> Dear John Doe:
>
> I got your name from the list of Amazon Top Reviewers. I've written a book, "How to Grow Organic Strawberries." I noticed from your Amazon profile that you frequently review gardening books. If you think you might be interested in reading my book and posting an honest review of it on Amazon, I'll gladly send a complimentary copy if you'll reply with your postal mailing address. There is no obligation, of course.
>
> Best Regards

Carefully screen out reviewers whose profile indicates they aren't interested in your book's topic. For example, don't send your fiction title to a reviewer whose profile says, "I review only nonfiction."

Some Amazon Top Reviewers make it a practice not to review a book from a new author unless they can honestly recommend it to others and give it a rating of at least three or four stars out of five.

Only a small portion of Top Reviewers are likely to respond to your offer. Some are inundated with review copies from publishers who already have their mailing address and know their reading preferences. Other Top Reviewers are skeptical of books sent directly from authors, after having received poorly written self-published books. Some busy Top Reviewers disable the Amazon Friend invitation system by adjusting their profile's privacy settings.

## Etiquette in approaching reviewers

Naturally, every author wants good reviews. And although it's perfectly ethical to seek reviews, don't do anything to suggest you're expecting favorable treatment. If you succeed in getting lots of reviews, you can expect some negative ones.

"I see a fair number of books that I don't like, and I say so—including those sent to me as review copies," says Jane Corn, one of Amazon's Top 150 reviewers. "Anything else seems unethical to me."

You can safeguard yourself a bit by requesting that Top Reviewers not post a review if they simply hate the book. But it's the reviewer's call. Sometimes reviewers are willing to give prepublication feedback, providing valuable advice on fixing a book's weaknesses. Don't expect that, though, and don't ask for it.

You might want to avoid sending your book to reviewers who usually post harshly negative reviews, but don't shy away from those who offer frank criticism. These voices lend credibility to your book, Corn says:

> " Readers are smart. They can figure out who to trust, and those are the reviewers you want to reach. Always be clear about your willingness to have a fair, honest review. Anything else is self-defeating.

## Finding more Amazon reviewers

Another valuable source of potential reviewers is people who've posted Amazon reviews for previous books in your topic or genre. You can contact them using the same techniques mentioned above. Click on the pen name displayed with their review to reach their Amazon profile, then use the Amazon Friends invitation to send a personalized message:

> Dear John Doe:
>
> I got your name from the Amazon book review you posted of the 2003 book "Complete Guide to Organic Fruit." I recently wrote a book that appeals to the same audience, "How to Grow Organic Strawberries." If you think you might be interested in reading it and perhaps reviewing it on Amazon, I'll gladly send a complimentary copy if you'll respond with your mailing address. There is no obligation, of course.
>
> Best Regards

These readers might not be frequent Amazon reviewers, but may consider it a treat to discover a new book in their field of interest. And there's another benefit of getting reviews from these specialized readers: Positive ratings from them can surface your book in Amazon's recommendations to buyers of similar books.

Finding volunteers to read and review your book is a long, tedious process but can be well worth the effort. If you spend two or three days inviting about 300 potential Amazon reviewers, you can expect to receive about 40 to 50 responses, and wind up with perhaps 35 reviews, a quite satisfactory result.

Remember that many folks are rightfully suspicious of e-mails that seem to promise something for nothing, and contain links to a Web site. Most users are still unfamiliar with the "Invitation to be an Amazon Friend," and often these messages are mistaken for spam, or simply deleted unread.

## More ways to get reviews

Once your book is selling, you'll have a steady stream of potential reviewers. Whenever you receive e-mails from readers with praise for your book or requests for further information, you might conclude your response this way:

> Thank you for the kind words about my book. If you ever have a spare moment, it would be a great help if you could post a review of it on Amazon and let other potential readers know why you liked it. It's not necessary to write a lengthy, formal review—a summary of the comments you sent me would be fine. Here's a link to the review form for my book:
>
> **http://www.Amazon.com/gp/customer-reviews/write-a-review.html?asin=ISBN**

The link at the end of the message takes the reader to Amazon's Web form for book reviews. To customize the link for your book, replace the last four characters, **ISBN**, with your book's ISBN numerals.

## Amazon Spotlight Reviews

Popular books on Amazon can draw dozens or even hundreds of reviews. But no matter how many reviews a book gets, two reviews have a special impact by design—a pair designated Spotlight Reviews. Amazon displays Spotlights above all others, sometimes permanently. Because they're usually the first bit of independent information buyers see about your book, Spotlights are crucial. Many browsers read only those two reviews before deciding whether to buy.

Spotlights don't appear until your book has several reviews posted. When your book is new, the first reviews appear about midway down your book's detail page. New reviews appear on top, bumping earlier reviews down a notch. When the sixth review appears, Amazon selects one review as a Spotlight and places it on top. After your book receives a few more reviews, another review is selected as the second Spotlight.

The selection process for Spotlight Reviews is automated. The review with the most "helpful" votes by customers usually gets the top spot, although reviews written by Top Reviewers carry more weight. Subsequent reviews appear in reverse chronological order below the Spotlight reviews. A maximum of six reviews appear on your book's detail page, along with a link to all previous reviews.

## Negative reviews

Positive reviews certainly help your book, but negative reviews on Amazon can have a bigger impact, according to a study published by the Yale School of Management. Multiple glowing reviews for a book tend to be dismissed by shoppers as "hype" generated by the author or publisher, the study found. Negative reviews, however, are taken more seriously because buyers usually believe they represent honest criticism from disappointed readers.

Buyers understand that no book pleases everyone, and that any book reviewed often enough will get an occasional thumbs-down. But in some cases, a single detailed, critical review can devastate sales on Amazon, particularly with nonfiction how-to books.

The study, *The Effect of Word of Mouth on Sales: Online Book Reviews* examined random titles from *Global Books in Print* and bestsellers from *Publishers Weekly*. You can read the entire study here:

**www.WeberBooks.com/reviews.pdf**

Early on, Amazon's decision to allow readers to post negative book reviews infuriated publishers, chief executive Jeff Bezos recalls:

> We had publishers writing to us, saying, "Why in the world would you allow negative reviews? Maybe you don't understand your business—you make money when you *sell* things. Get rid of the negative reviews, and leave the positive ones."

Yes, negative reviews can hurt sales in the short term, but over the long term, allowing criticism builds credibility and helps shoppers decide what to buy, Bezos says: "We don't make money when we sell things, we make money when we help people make purchase decisions."

**Figure 3.1**

## How one negative review can hurt book sales

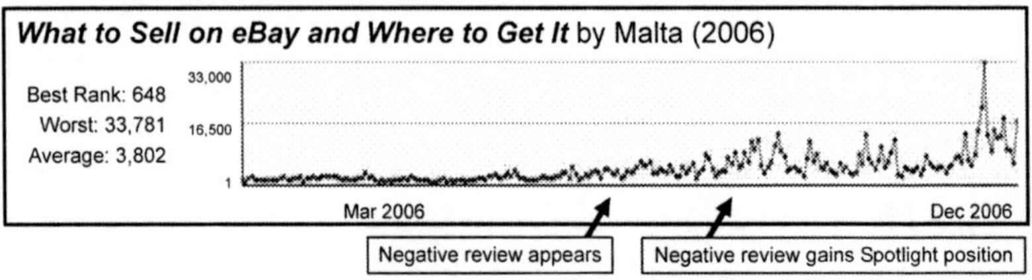


This how-to book, published in January 2006, had very strong sales and overwhelmingly positive customer reviews on Amazon for its first six months. Then, a harshly negative review appeared in June 2006 that seemed to effectively question the book's value. Immediately, sales slumped, shown here by the rising line indicating a worsening Amazon Sales Rank.

Over the next several weeks, Amazon users who read the negative review consistently voted it "helpful," causing it to rise to the top Spotlight Review position. This made the negative review much more visible to casual shoppers and bolstered its credibility. Sales weakened further.

Certainly, it's not unusual for sales to taper off three to six months after a book's publication. In this case, however, sales began deteriorating immediately after the negative review and worsened as the review gained visibility.

What's the lesson for authors and publishers? Ask for reviews. The more often your book is reviewed, the less likely that a minority opinion can dominate. Numerous authentic reviews lessen the chance that a single review can overtake and monopolize the Spotlight position.

Niche nonfiction and instructional books seem particularly vulnerable to a single, devastating review. Other books are less review-driven, especially political and religious tomes. Conservative pundit Ann Coulter's books are clobbered daily with nasty reviews but sell like hotcakes. Kevin Trudeau's book *Natural Cures* has had monster sales on Amazon for nearly three years, even though many reviewers attack the author and argue that his book is merely an advertisement for his subscription Web site.

---

# Countering malicious reviews

Amazon polices its book review system but depends on community members to report abuses. Because Amazon reviews can be posted anonymously, nothing prevents the occasional malicious review or practical joke. In one well-known case, a prankster ridiculed Microsoft, then signed the review "Bill Gates," the name of the company's founder.

Familiarize yourself with Amazon's guidelines for acceptable reviews so you can request that its Community Help department delete inappropriate reviews. Generally, Amazon requires reviews to critique the book itself. Reviews that focus on the author or outside topics are often deleted.

Amazon also deletes reviews deemed “illegal, obscene, threatening, defamatory, invasive of privacy, infringing of intellectual property rights, or otherwise injurious to third parties.” It also prohibits “political campaigning, commercial solicitation, chain letters, mass mailings, or any form of ‘spam.’”

Reviewers are prohibited from impersonating other persons or using profanity, obscenities, spiteful remarks, phone numbers, mail addresses, URLs, product pricing and availability, alternative ordering or shipping information, or solicitations for helpful “votes” for reviews. Amazon has also been known to delete negative reviews posted by competing authors, reviews that contain inaccurate information about the author or publisher, and off-topic reviews.

You can request deletion of an inappropriate review on Amazon by sending an e-mail to **community-help@amazon.com**. Specify the book title, ISBN, the pen name of the reviewer, the first sentence of the review, and the date it was posted. State why you believe the review is inappropriate, and you should receive a reply within a few days.

Sometimes authors themselves abuse Amazon’s review system. More on this later.

## Old-media book reviews

Most newspapers and magazines have reduced space for book reviews in recent years, even as the number of books published has skyrocketed. Many of the remaining review columns are syndicated by national writers, leaving little opportunity for new authors to get reviewed, even in local media.

The long odds of getting reviewed don’t deter many authors, and traditional media outlets are being bombarded with self-published books. However, most old-media reviewers simply won’t consider a book unless it’s from a major trade publisher.

Sometimes feature sections of newspapers—such as the Lifestyle, Home, or Business sections—are more likely to feature a book, particularly one by a local author.

One drawback to distributing review copies of your book is that many of them will quickly appear for sale on Amazon Marketplace, even if you stamp “Review Copy, Not For Sale” on the front cover. Although

Amazon's policies prohibit the sale of review copies, it still occurs, and of course you'll receive no revenue from those sales.

You certainly don't want to refuse a legitimate request for a review copy. But a more realistic strategy for obtaining reviews in print media is to target specialized magazines and trade publications in your niche. You can find such publications by consulting the *Gale Directory of Publications and Broadcast Media*, available in many larger libraries. Another valuable resource is the Gebbie Press *All-In-One Media Directory*, which lists 24,000 outlets, including newspapers, magazines and radio stations. You can purchase and download lists of contacts at **www.GebbieInc.com**.

If more than three months remain before your book's publication date, you can submit it for consideration in these trade review publications:

**Booklist:**
Ala.org/booklist/submit.html
800-545-2433

**Kirkus Reviews:**
www.Kirkusreviews.com/kirkusreviews/about_us/submission.jsp
212-777-4554

**Library Journal:**
www.LibraryJournal.com/info/CA603906.html
212-463-6823

**Publishers Weekly:**
www.PublishersWeekly.com/index.asp?layout=submissions
212-645-9700

**Midwest Book Review:**
www.midwestbookreview.com/get_rev.htm
608-835-7937

Self-published authors get special consideration from Midwest Book Review, which also gives special preference to small presses and members of the Publishers Marketing Association. If your book is selected, its review will be posted to online retailers, relevant Web sites and forums, and included on an interactive CD-ROM provided to corporate, academic, and public library systems.

## Posting trade reviews on Amazon

Amazon licenses prepublication reviews from major trade publications, so if you have secured these reviews, ensure they appear on your title's Amazon detail page. For reviews published in newspapers or other publications for which Amazon doesn't license reprints, you can condense the review to 20 words and Amazon will republish the summary on your book's detail page relying on the "fair use" exemption of copyright law.

Amazon will display a maximum of 10 published reviews on your book's detail page. For information on submitting reviews and other descriptive content about your book to Amazon, see:

**www.Amazon.com/publishers**

## Fee-based book reviews

Considering the work involved in getting book reviews, more authors than ever are willing to pay for them. Several fee-based review services have popped up in recent years, primarily to serve self-publishing authors who are effectively locked out of traditional book reviews.

Many publishers believe paid reviews are ineffective and unethical, but that hasn't stopped a variety of companies from offering them, even publishers of respected library journals such as Kirkus and Bowker. Reviews on Bowker's BookWire site cost $295. The review is posted at www.BookWire.com and you receive a PDF copy of the review, which you can submit to newspapers or enclose in other promotional materials. For information, e-mail **charlie.friscia@bowker.com**.

Kirkus Discoveries reviews cost $350 and are sent to the publisher as a PDF and posted at www.KirkusDiscoveries.com. There's also Kirkus Reports, a compilation of paid reviews sent via e-mail to anyone who subscribes. Publishers pay $95 per title. You can sign up to receive this and other Kirkus newsletters at:

**www.Kirkusreviews.comkirkusreviews/newsletter/email.jsp**

Another fee-based review service is operated by Foreword Magazine at **www.ForewordMagazine.com/clarion**. An online review costs $305, and the company makes it available in key databases used by booksellers and librarians—Bowker's Books-In-Print online, Baker & Taylor's Titlesource 3, and Ingram's iPage.

Critics argue these paid reviews aren't read by consumers, and that their supposed target audience—booksellers and librarians—pay no attention to paid reviews.

"I feel that paying for book reviews is a bad idea," says self-publishing guru Dan Poynter. "There's a compromise there. And people can see right through it—they know it's a paid review, so it's an ad."

Jim Cox, editor in chief of Midwest Book Review, puts it this way:

> Any reviewer that wants money from you for any purpose whatsoever is operating a scam, engaging in unethical behavior that is in violation of the publishing industry etiquette and norm.

# Building your author Web site

Few people can benefit more from a Web site than authors. A simple do-it-yourself site can provide a huge visibility boost at very low cost.

Before you begin planning your site, consider your target audience and what type of information you want to give them. Will your site be a topic-driven site, or a personality-driven site? Topic-driven sites usually work best for nonfiction, and if you continue writing related books, you'll have a built-in audience for those new books. Personality-driven sites can work well for fiction writers and those with famous names.

Whatever your approach, the goal is to provide content your target audience finds worthwhile.

## Getting involved

Some authors outsource their Web project, paying a designer $500 or more to build what amounts to an online brochure. That's a big mistake, because static Web sites with little content don't draw the repeat traffic that will sell your book.

Although it may seem like a daunting technical challenge, building your own site is easier than ever, thanks to improved software tools. Every major Internet hosting company now offers a variety of design templates you can use to start quickly, without having to learn computer coding. You'll gain much more from your Web site if you're the one maintaining it.

Three basic options exist for those establishing their first author site:

- **Do it yourself** by registering a domain name and building your own site. This option requires you to learn a few software tools, but provides more flexibility and control. **GoDaddy.com** offers fast, reliable service, and a wide variety of Web domain registration and hosting plans at competitive prices. There's no setup fee and no annual commitment is required. GoDaddy's economy plan includes 5 gigabytes of disk space, 500 e-mail accounts, forums, blogging, and photo galleries for $3.99 a month. This hosting company and most competitors such as **www.Register.com** offer simple tools and templates for building your own site.

- **Using a free account** at a network such as MySpace.com, Google Pages, Blogger.com, or LiveJournal.com. A packaged solution like this is easy to learn, but provides less flexibility. Some sites feature advertising you can't control, which can distract visitors from your message.

- **Consulting a Web designer** through your local Yellow Pages, or an online firm that specializes in designing author sites. For example, **www.AuthorsOnTheWeb.com** offers professional designs starting at $2,500. For additional fees the company will set up and maintain extras like audio, video, or a blog. A cheaper option is **www.AmericanAuthor.com**, which charges a $299 setup fee and $29 monthly for a base plan. Another choice is **www.Authors-Online.com**.

One way to get started quickly while preserving your future options is to pay GoDaddy or another registrar $9 to register your own domain, such as **www.YourBookTitle.com** or **www.YourName.com**, then forward the traffic to your account at MySpace, Blogger, or others. Later, if you choose to build a dedicated site, you can forward the traffic there. This strategy allows you to start building your online audience without the risk of losing readers if you switch your focus to another site.

In any case, it's prudent to make backup copies of all content you post to a free account on sites like Blogger or MySpace, since these free accounts are sometimes deleted accidentally.

Google Pages is an easy, free tool you can use to create Web pages quickly without having to learn HTML code. Google will host up to 100 megabytes of Web pages at no charge. To open a free account, see **www.Pages.Google.com**.

## Your domain

If you're committed to actively supporting your book, it's best to stake out your own territory on the Web. This means registering your own domain name, which you alone control. GoDaddy.com,

Register.com and NetworkSolutions.com are well known, reliable firms where you can buy a package of services—domain registration, Web hosting, and e-mail accounts.

You may want to use the title of your book as the domain. Authors with more than one book often register a new domain for each book, or simply use a different folder on their site for each book, such as **www.JaneDoe.com/Book1** and **www.JaneDoe.com/Book2**.

Keep your domain name short and memorable so people who see it or hear of it can recall it. Hyphenated domain names are usually a bad idea—they're harder to remember and they fail the "radio test" because they're difficult to repeat in conversation.

## Building blocks of your site

The great thing about a Web site is you can always add to it. Here are some basic elements you'll want to consider adding to your site:

- Content. Nobody will visit a site that's merely an advertisement for your book. Your content can be a series of articles, book excerpts, or even feedback from your readers.
- Book cover artwork, description, and excerpts.
- Your biography.
- Links to purchase your book, either on your site or online retailers such as Amazon and Barnes & Noble. The more choices you offer buyers, the better.
- Reviews of your book.
- A form where visitors can enter their e-mail address to subscribe to a newsletter or site updates.
- Contact information—your e-mail address (or a form that forwards messages) and perhaps postal address and phone number.
- A "media room" with any press releases announcing your book or any news coverage involving you or your book.
- Suggested interview questions, along with your responses.

## A survey of author Web sites

Every author site is different, and you're free to borrow ideas from the best, and ignore the worst. Here are some good examples:

**www.Scottoline.com**

This feature-packed site of mystery writer **Lisa Scottoline** includes everything the newcomer or longtime fan might want: a biography and several photos, background stories on her books, links to buy the books at various online retailers, book club information, tour schedules, an e-mail newsletter sign-up form, monthly trivia contests, audio and video clips of interviews, order forms for tote bags and signed bookplates, and a media kit with press releases and high-resolution photos. For each of Scottoline's 13 titles, visitors to the site can view the cover art, reviews, and the first chapter.

Although this site is designed and maintained by specialists, it illustrates features any do-it-yourselfer can emulate on their own site.

**www.CrapHound.com**

Award-winning science-fiction writer **Cory Doctorow** maintains this site himself. The main page is a diary-style list of updates about Doctorow's travels, interviews, and current articles. From a navigation bar at the top of the main page, visitors can dig into Doctorow's novels, nonfiction books, and articles he's written for newspapers and magazines. Other sections include a biography and a recurring audio clip of Doctorow reading from one of his stories each week, called a *podcast*.

In one section of the site, **www.CrapHound.com/unwirer**, readers can view a story that was written online, a collaboration of Doctorow and author Charlie Stross. The story was written in public using a blog, with the whole process exposed to the public, so anyone could see and participate in the writing.

Doctorow publishes his site using the WordPress blogging system. Interestingly, Doctorow allows visitors to download the full text of any of his books for free. He believes the resulting word of mouth outweighs the danger of any lost sales.

**www.Freakonomics.com**

Like most good author sites, this one has a clean, uncluttered design. Reading a Web site is made easier with the liberal use of white space.

Built to support the 2005 business bestseller, Freakonomics.com includes links to more information about the book, news stories covering topics in the book, and new articles by the book's co-authors. Free signed bookplates are offered to visitors who register their name and address.

Free downloadable teaching guides are available for instructors who assign the book to college and high school students. And of course, there are links to buy the book at online retailers.

This popular site helped build an audience for expanded editions in hardcover and paperback, and is piquing interest in a planned sequel, *SuperFreakonomics*.

This site is simple but well planned. For example, many folks misspell the book's title as *Freakanomics*. Realizing this, the publisher also reserved a domain for the misspelling, and those who type the wrong name into their Web browser are forwarded here.

**www.SethGodin.com**

Here's a site that's constantly updated to feature the latest business book by bestselling author **Seth Godin**. From this page, visitors are a link or two away from Godin's popular blog, a calendar of his public appearances, and links to his other books.

Godin displays generous samples of his books, and for one of his bestsellers, *Unleashing the Ideavirus*, allows visitors to download the entire text free:

**www.IdeaVirus.com**.

**www.DavidLouisEdelman.com/jump225/infoquake**

Here's a do-it-yourself site by a first-time novelist, **David Louis Edelman**. It includes book excerpts, forums, a blog, biography, and free audio of Edelman reading from the book. Visitors can also subscribe to announcements of book signings and readings.

Edelman provides a level of detail that few others match. For example, each of his nine Chapter 1 drafts are posted on the site, along with footnotes recounting the editorial decisions made for each draft.

Although Edelman is an experienced Web designer, he contends that anyone with basic computer skills can build an author site similar to his using simple, inexpensive tools like Google Pages and WordPress, a blog service.

**www.AaronShep.com**

In 1996 **Aaron Shepard** was one of the first children's authors to venture onto the Web. His site provides teachers, librarians, storytellers, and parents with a collection of free reader's theater scripts. Shepard provides stories in adaptations for storytellers, and in their original form for normal reading. The site has led to a number of subsidiary and foreign rights deals.

Other areas of Shepard's site are geared toward adults interested in writing and publishing. One handy resource is this tutorial on creating short, simple Web links to your books on Amazon:

**www.AaronShep.com/publishing/AmazonLinking.html**

## Your online press kit

In addition to showcasing your writing, a Web site enables you to host publicity materials at practically no cost. Instead of sending press releases and photographs via overnight mail, you can make the material available immediately to anyone.

Online press kits usually include an author biography, book descriptions and artwork, book excerpts, and high-resolution photographs suitable for reproduction in print publications. Some authors include a sample interview, with "suggested" questions and answers.

Here's an excellent example of an online author press kit:

**www.TLHines.com/presskit.html**

The kit includes PDF documents of press releases for the release of each book, suggested interview questions and answers, and a page of "interesting facts" about the author and his latest title. Several high-resolution photographs of the author in black-and-white and color are offered, suitable for reproduction in newspapers or magazines.

Here's an online press kit for author David Baldacci:

**www.DavidBaldacci.com/press**

And here, Baldacci provides the "Top 10" questions he's asked most often in interviews:

**www.DavidBaldacci.com/faq**

Some authors choose not to dedicate a specific area of their site to a press room. According to their theory, "publicity" materials are interesting to readers as well as the media, providing an "insider" feel. Instead of an online press room, these authors have a variety of pages dedicated to "touring," "photos," "biography," and other content.

## Multimedia for books

As high-speed Internet service becomes more common, audio and video content are becoming valuable tools for online book promotion. Multimedia is particularly effective for niche authors and newcomers who haven't attracted mainstream media coverage.

Multimedia grabs the attention of younger people who spend more leisure time online, while consuming less traditional media like newspapers and television. Meanwhile, production and distribution of trailers is getting easier and cheaper by the day, thanks to inexpensive video cameras and free hosting sites like **www.YouTube.com**.

*Book trailers*, an increasingly popular tool for book publicity, often resemble movie previews, music videos or talk shows. Even though trailers are promotional materials, the people who choose to watch often perceive them as interesting, valuable content.

For authors and publishers, trailers can serve as an infomercial, a message that appears on a cable network of 5 million channels—except you have global reach and very low costs. The videos contain a "buy this book" link to Amazon or the publisher's site, prompting impulse purchases from viewers, which can make an effective trailer instantly profitable.

**www.VidLit.com** produces slick, relatively expensive trailers using animation, narration and background music. The clips can be hosted on the author's blog or Web site, or e-mailed to newsletter subscribers. As part of its service, VidLit.com can forward trailers to literary bloggers who often post the video on their blogs.

Successful trailers are an example of *viral marketing* because of the huge exposure gained through Web links and e-mails. Thanks largely to e-mail forwarding, a trailer for the humor book *Yiddish with Dick and Jane* was seen by 1 million people during its first week, helping to sell 150,000 copies of the book. You can view the video at:

**www.Vidlit.com/yidlit**

The videos usually last a few minutes, using Flash animation, providing a razor-sharp picture. You can view company founder Liz Dubelman's own explanation of how she started producing book trailers at:

**www.Vidlit.com/editor**

VidLit also has a more modest product called the Naked Author Series. A four-minute question-and-answer session is recorded by telephone with the author, who receives a disposable camera with 48 exposures. Whatever snapshots the author takes—their book, their goldfish, a potted plant—are woven into the trailer.

Trailers for fiction books sometimes resemble movie previews. The video for *Shadow Man*, a thriller about a female FBI agent, has no dialogue at all, just images of a police raid, a distraught woman holding her child, and a suspicious-looking man hiding in the background. You can view this video and other award-winners at:

**www.TheBookStandard.com/bookstandard/ events/book_video/index.jsp**

Skeptics point out that slick videos can confuse viewers, who might assume they're watching a movie clip instead of a book promotion. And there's the expense—firms like VidLit charge $10,000 for production of a single video, making it beyond the reach of most first-time or niche authors. However, for books with a marketing budget, a trailer can cost far less than an advertisement in a trade publication, while delivering more eyeballs.

Other trailer producers include **BookShorts.com**, **BookWrap-Central.com**, and **TeachingBooks.net**, a producer of short documentaries on books used in schools.

**www.AuthorViews.com** takes a leaner approach, simply taping authors talking about their books. The premise is, authors are the best spokespeople for their work, and readers are curious to know what their favorite writers look and sound like. The price is certainly right—free. The company tours major cities and provides free taping, using student film crews and interns to keep costs low. The company takes revenue from donations, sponsorships and advertising.

Do-it-yourself videos are another option, thanks to falling prices of digital camcorders. Video clips are an effective tool for authors unable to finance a bookstore tour, or whose disparate audience makes touring impractical. If you have a PC with Windows XP, you can edit digital video yourself using a free program in your Accessories folder called "Movie Maker." If you're a Mac user, there's iMovie.

Author Chris Epting scored big using YouTube to promote his 2007 book *Led Zeppelin Crashed Here*, a guide to "rock and roll landmarks." Six months before publication, Epting began posting a series of trailers, featuring photos he shot for the book backed with classic-rock soundtracks. The videos prompted thousands of rock fans to write to Epting with suggestions for the book and requests to buy it. Closer to his publication date, Epting posted interactive videos and a trivia contest. You can view the videos here:

**www.youtube.com/view_play_list?p=FA5F436AF546723F**

## Podcasting for publicity

A podcast is an audio file hosted on the Web, available to listeners anytime. Audio recordings you may already have—such as interviews or book-readings—can be repurposed as a podcast, providing Internet users with yet another way to discover you and your book.

Some podcasts are a recurring feature, sometimes called a podiobook. Perhaps you'll decide to provide your audio content for free to help generate word of mouth for your book. Some authors create value-added podcasts and charge subscription fees.

Readers can listen to your podcasts on their PCs, or download them to a portable music player such as an iPod. The word *podcast* is a combination of the word iPod and broadcasting, but no iPod is required—anyone with speakers on their computer can listen.

Just like blog-reading provides insights for building your own blog, listening to podcasts will inspire ideas for producing your own audio content. Here are some directories where you can sample what's available:

- **iTunes:** www.Apple.com/itunes/podcasts. Here you can sample or subscribe to podcasts.
- **Yahoo Podcasts:** Podcasts.yahoo.com. Listen to podcasts using your Web browser, or download files.
- **PodioCast:** PodioCast.com. Serialized audiobooks.
- **LibriVox:** Librivox.org. Free audiobooks from the public domain.

To record material for your podcasts, all that's required is a microphone and PC. Free software for recording and editing podcasts is offered at **www.Audacity.Sourceforge.net**. Another option is **www.HipCast.com**, which lets you create podcasts through your Web browser or telephone, then post it to your blog or Web site. For Mac users, GarageBand is a good podcast tool.

Here's a guide for making your own podcasts:

**www.How-To-Podcast-Tutorial.com**

## Waiting for results

Building a Web site can be a lonely process, much like the early phases of writing a manuscript. Don't expect a big response in the first month or even the next six months. Often it takes an entire year for an author site or blog to gain momentum. But if you concentrate on producing a useful site with quality content, word will get around.

As you build your site, keep one general idea in mind: Unless you're already a superstar, don't make your Web site about *you*. Make it about *the reader*. Provide compelling content that solves problems, entertains, sparks curiosity, or inspires. Everything else will follow.

Resist the temptation to pack your site with fancy features like flashy graphics or voices or music that plays automatically. Usually these doodads have the opposite effect than what was intended—they make your site slow, irritating, noisy and hard to read.

## When to launch your site

Launch your site as soon as you can. It's impossible to be too early, and it's never too late. By all means, don't wait until your book's publication date. Having a Web site is not only a valuable tool for publicizing a book, but for writing a book too. More on that later.

"The best time to start promoting your book is three years before it comes out," says bestselling author Seth Godin. "Three years to build a reputation, build a permission asset, build a blog, build a following, build credibility, and build the connections you'll need later."

# Blogging for authors

Julie Powell moved to New York to become an actress. A few years later, she realized she was 30 years old, working a dead-end job to pay the bills, and still had no acting prospects. Then, on a visit to Texas, she borrowed her mother's copy of Julia Child's landmark 1961 cookbook, *Mastering the Art of French Cooking, Volume 1*. Back in her cramped kitchen on Long Island, Powell cooked one of the recipes for her husband, who enjoyed it so much he urged her to attend culinary school and become a professional cook.

Instead, Powell decided to teach herself, and let the whole world watch. She vowed to cook each of the book's 524 recipes during the following year, and write a diary about it on a Web log, or *blog*. Powell wrote about killing lobsters, boiling calves hooves, and making homemade mayonnaise, but she didn't confine herself to cooking. For good measure, she heaped on details of her sex life, recipes for reviving a romance, and snide remarks about her backstabbing coworkers.

As Powell began one entry: "My husband almost divorced me last night, and it was all because of the sauce tartar." Her storytelling was so good, word got around fast and thousands began reading her blog—regardless of whether they cared about French cuisine. A write-up in the New York Times brought thousands more readers.

By the time Powell was winding down her project, publishers were knocking on the door with book contracts, and her blog turned into the bestseller *Julie and Julia: 365 Days, 524 Recipes, 1 Tiny Apartment Kitchen*. More than 100,000 copies sold its first year, a monster success for any memoir, let alone a book by an unknown, chronically unemployed actress.

Here's a humorous online trailer featuring Powell chatting about the book and how it happened:

**www.Blip.tv/file/78726**

Blogging is a relatively easy way for you to publicize your book and even improve your writing while you're at it. If you can write an e-mail, you can write a blog—it's the easiest, cheapest, and perhaps best way for authors to find an audience and connect with readers. Blogging is an informal, intimate form of communication that inspires trust among your readers.

For the same reasons that traditional advertising is usually ineffective for selling books, a blog can be highly effective for book promotion. People interested in your topic seek out your message.

## What is a blog?

Put simply, a blog is a Web site with a few interactive features. You don't have to call it a blog unless you want to. It's possible that within a few years, nearly every Web site will have interactive features, and people simply won't call them blogs anymore.

You needn't know anything about computers to blog. Simply type into a form, and presto—the whole world can see it. Your blog is a *content management* system—a painless way to build and maintain a platform where readers can discover and enjoy your writing.

A blog can be a part of your Web site, or it can be *the* Web site. The main thing that distinguishes a blog from a plain old Web site is that a blog is frequently updated with short messages, or *posts*. Readers often chime in with their own comments at the bottom of each post. This free exchange of ideas is what makes blogs a revolutionary tool for authors: A successful blog is a constant stream of ideas, inspiration, perspective, and advice—it's a real-time, global focus group.

## Why blogs are better

Some authors who already have a book for sale resist the idea of blogging and the "extra work" it entails. Their reasoning is, "Why create more deadlines when your book is already finished?" Well, blogging can help you maximize the effectiveness of things you're probably already doing, like answering e-mails from your readers.

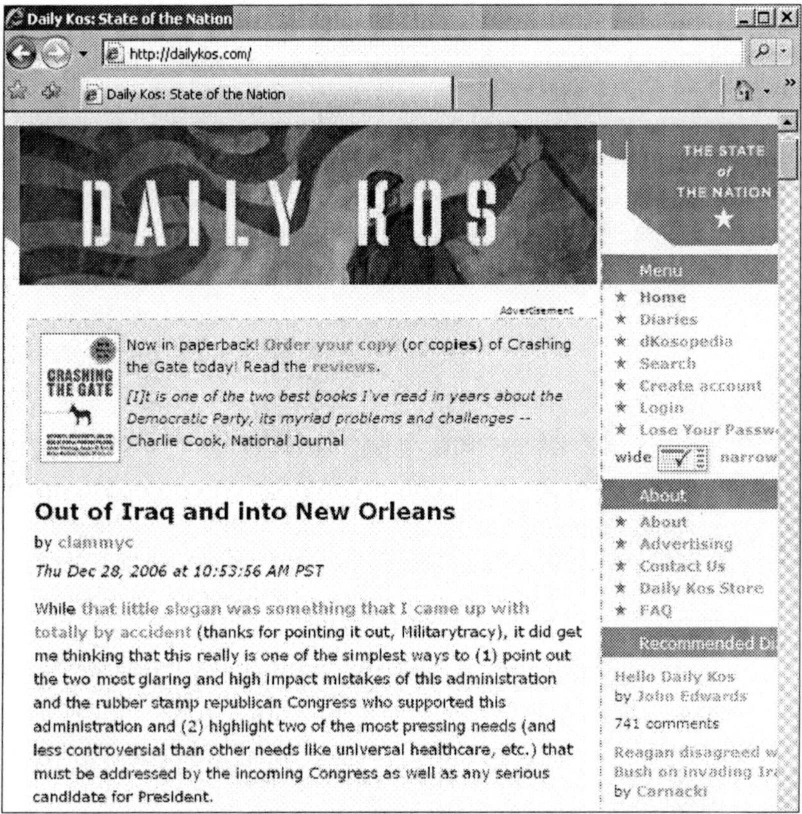


A popular political blog, Daily Kos.

Compared with other types of Internet publicity content such as static Web sites or e-mail newsletters, blogs provide three big advantages:

- Blogs are easy to start and maintain.
- The short, serialized content of blogs encourages regular readership, repeated exposure to your books, and more sales.
- Blogs rank high in search-engine results from Google and other providers, making them easy to find.

Why do blogs get so much traffic from search engines? First, blogs are topical. When you're writing about the same topics and ideas day in and day out, your site becomes packed with the keywords your audience is searching for. Stay at it awhile, and it becomes nearly impossible for your target audience to miss you, thanks to Google and the other search engines. Most new visitors will find your site by using a search engine, after looking for words and topics contained in your Web pages.

Another reason blogs are so easy to find is that search engines usually rank them higher than other types of Web sites. Thus your links can show up at the top of search results, which is where most people click.

Google and the other search engines give extra credit to blogs for a couple of reasons:

- Blogs are updated frequently, and the assumption is "fresh" content is more valuable.
- Blogs tend to have many links from other Web pages with similar content. The assumption is that because other bloggers and Webmasters have decided to link to your content, it's probably valuable.

Your visibility in search results is key, since about 40 percent of your new visitors will likely arrive via a Web search. If your site ranks highly in Web searches for the keywords related to your book, you'll have a constant source of well-qualified visitors and likely book buyers.

## Breathing the blogosphere

Step 1 in becoming a blogger is to consume some blogs yourself. Reading other blogs gives you a quick feel for what works, what doesn't, and the techniques you'll want to apply to your own blog.

There are millions of blogs, and finding ones that suit you can be like searching for a needle in a haystack. There's no easy way to filter out low-quality blogs—you've just got to sample what's out there.

A good place to begin is by browsing for blogs about your hobbies, pastimes and passions. You can find a list of the most popular blogs here:

**www.Technorati.com/pop/blogs**

You can drill down into niche territory by browsing **www.Technorati.com/blogs**, where you'll find a menu of subjects on the left. You can also search blogs by keyword at these sites:

**www.Blogsearch.Google.com**
**www.Feedster.com**
**www.IceRocket.com**

Once you've found a few blogs of interest, it's easy to find more. Bloggers tend to link to one another, both within their blog posts, and often within a side menu of links known as a *blogroll.*

A handy tool for keeping track of all your blogs is a *newsreader* or *aggregator*, which saves you the trouble of poking around the Web, looking for new blog posts. Instead, your newsreader gathers and displays updates for you. One free, easy-to-use reader is:

**www.Bloglines.com**

You'll quickly learn which blogs you've subscribed to are must-reads, and which can be ignored or deleted.

## Connecting with readers

It's natural to be apprehensive about starting a blog. When you first begin, it may feel like being on stage without a script or a view of the audience. Don't worry, feedback will come soon enough. Remember, there's no right or wrong way to blog. The only rule is your target audience must find something worthwhile.

One way to ease into blogging is to start with a temporary blog at **www.Blogger.com**, where you can set up a free practice blog in five minutes. Take a dry run for a week or two, then make your blog public when you're ready.

Good blogs are addictive, which is one reason they're so effective for authors. Many book buyers must be exposed to a title six or seven times before deciding to buy. With a good blog, getting repeated exposure won't be a problem.

A lively blog is like a focus group and writing laboratory rolled into one: It provides you with constant feedback, criticism, and new ideas. Your blog readers will pepper you with comments and e-mails. When you've struck a chord, you'll know immediately from the response. When you lay an egg, you'll know that too, from the silence.

Just as theater companies try out new productions in the hinterlands before storming Broadway, authors can fine tune their material on their blog, says technology writer Clive Thompson:

> "Ask writers who blog regularly—like me—and they'll tell you how exciting it is to be wired in directly to your audience. They correspond with you, pass you tips, correct your factual blunders, and introduce you to brilliant new ideas and people. The Internet isn't just an audience, it's an auxiliary brain. But you have to turn it on, and it takes work. You can't fake participation and authenticity online.

Indeed, the true power of blogging is the momentum created by your audience. Once your blog has 100 frequent readers, it has critical mass. It may take six months or a year to get there, but from there it's all downhill. Members of your core audience begin competing to hand you the most useful, compelling ideas by writing comments on your blog and e-mailing you directly. That's when your blog becomes electric, a magnet attracting new readers. Your core audience swells as word of mouth goes viral.

# Blog comments: pros and cons

Most blogs include space below the author's posts for readers to add their own views. These comments can take the conversation in a totally new direction, and become the most interesting material on your blog, thanks purely to your readers' efforts.

For the blogger, comments bring three key benefits:

- Instant feedback on your ideas and writing, and a sense of what your audience finds valuable.
- Feeling of participation and loyalty among your audience.
- Adding valuable keyword density to your site, making it much more visible in search-engine results.

Like any tool, however, comments can be abused. It's not unusual to see rude or off-topic comments on some blogs, and even "spam comments" written solely to plant links back to the spammer's site. The worst spammers even use software robots, which scour the Web for target blogs and insert their junk links. Spam comments are usually along the lines of, "Hey, great blog. Come see us at **www.Cheap-Viagra.com**."

Fortunately, most problem comments can be prevented by using countermeasures like *comment moderation*: you review and approve new comments before they appear on your blog. Another option is to allow readers to post comments immediately, and you review them later. The advantage is your readers get immediate gratification in seeing their comments posted as they submit them.

Most spam comments can be prevented by using *word verification*, requiring comment writers to type a short series of characters displayed in an image. This stops spam comments from software robots.

To be sure, some popular authors don't allow blog comments at all, such as marketing guru Seth Godin. Simply because they're well known, famous writers attract a certain number of crackpots and sycophants, and perhaps it's easier to avoid them by allowing no comments.

## Blog style

Just as every book and author is unique, there's an endless variety of blog styles and flavors. All the blogging services have page templates, allowing you to start with a basic design and add a few personal elements.

Don't get bogged down looking for the "perfect" design. You'll always be free to tweak your design later, or do a complete overhaul. The most important thing is to get started adding content and building your audience.

The main design requirement is readability. Plain vanilla blogs are fine, and are actually preferred by most readers—it's the words that count. Black text on a white background might seem uninspired, but it's much easier on the eyes than white text on a black background or some other color. A plain masthead, simply your blog title in capital letters, is fine to start. The important thing is to get started.

## Your blog's angle

A nonfiction author's blog can approach the topic from several directions:

- New developments.
- New products or services.
- Hot-button issues of the day.
- What other blogs or media are saying.
- Reviews of new books in the field.

You can publish a blog in the style of a perpetual newsletter, an aggregation of interesting tidbits about your book's topic. As you notice new things and write about them, each post is stacked on top, and with each new post added on top, one of the older posts is bumped from the bottom and sent to your archives.

Let's imagine you're writing a blog on the topic of *Organic Strawberries*. Your blog could serve as an information clearinghouse covering every conceivable angle and trend of organic strawberry growing, cooking, and consuming. You'll constantly monitor consumer and trade media for the latest news on organic growing, interpret this material for your audience, and link to the source material, adding your own commentary.

Your blog could include:

- Questions from your blog readers on organic fruit, along with your answers.
- Guest articles from experts on organic strawberry gardening.
- New books and magazines on the topic.
- Strawberry dessert recipes.
- The best places to grow organic strawberries.
- Listings and maps of markets offering organic strawberries.
- Reviews of cookbooks addressing natural, organic, fruit and dessert preparation.

Fiction authors have even more freedom, but a bigger creative burden. They can write about themselves, or even from the point of view of a fictional character. A story from their book can continue on the blog, veering off in new directions, experimentally, in response to suggestions from readers and other writers.

## Raw materials for posts

A free, easy way to find new raw material for your blog is to create a *Google Alert*, which will automatically scour thousands of media sources for any keywords you specify. You'll be alerted via e-mail when something containing your keywords appears in newspapers, magazines, Web sites, or other sources. Sign up at:

**www.Google.com/alerts**

Google Alerts are also a handy way to monitor mentions of your blog title, book titles, and even your name or the names of other authors.

## Your blog's title

A blog title usually spans the top portion of each page like a newspaper masthead. Titles are usually short and catchy—perhaps just a couple of nonsense words like *Boing Boing*, or a made-up compound word like *RocketBoom* or *BuzzMachine*. The name could be a non sequitur or double-entendre like PostSecret. Sometimes a title is just a title, like *The Official Google Weblog*.

Try to include in your title the most critical keyword related to your niche. *Joe's Organic Strawberry Growing, Baking and Eating Guide* is a good title. A poor title would be *Joe's Thoughts and Ideas about Fruit* because nobody would search for something like that, and if they saw it, they couldn't guess what it's about. Be obvious. Pick a few words that will be easy for people to remember and to repeat in conversation and e-mails.

## Writing your blog posts

The essential ingredient of a blog is its short entries, or posts. They're arranged in reverse chronological order, with the newest at top.

Posts can be a few sentences long, or many paragraphs long, and often link to outside information like blogs, newspaper stories, or multimedia clips hosted elsewhere on the Web.

Nearly any tidbit of information relevant to your audience can be spun into a blog post of some type:

- **Informational.** A news-oriented blurb. A new development.
- **Question/Answer.** Easy to write, and fun to read. Reliable material, even if you have to make up the question.
- **Instructional**. Can be a longer post, a tutorial that explains how to do something related to your niche.
- **Link posts.** Find an interesting blog post elsewhere. Link to it and add your own spin.
- **Rant.** Let off some steam, and let it rip. Interesting blogs don't play it safe, they take sides.
- **Book review.** Review a book related to your field. It can be a new book or a classic that newcomers haven't heard of.
- **Product reviews.** The word "review" is a popular search term. Give your frank opinion, and encourage your readers to chime in with their own views.
- **Lists**. Write about the "Top 5 Ways" to do a task, or the "Top 10 Reasons" for such-and-such. Readers love lists. If someone else publishes a list, you can summarize it or critique it on your own blog.
- **Interviews**. Chat with someone in your field. Provide a text summary on your blog. You can also add a transcript or even an audio file.
- **Case studies.** Report on how so-and-so does such-and-such. You don't have to call it a "case study," just tell the story.
- **Profiles**. Profiles focus on a particular person, a personality. The person profiled can be someone well known in your field, or perhaps a newcomer nobody's heard of.

Most blogs are conversational and informal, but that doesn't give authors a license to be sloppy. Readers expect clear writing from an author, and that requires attention to detail—not to mention beginning your sentences with capital letters and ending them with periods. It's worth proofreading and spell-checking your posts before publishing. Keeping your paragraphs short will minimize your rewriting chores.

## Blogging categories

One helpful feature for you and your readers is blog categories. Assign each post to one or more categories, such as "technology," "marketing," "features," "reviews," or however you can best divide your material. Category headings can be listed on your blog's margin, and are especially valuable for new readers.

Assigning your posts to category headings can be especially handy later for your own writing tasks—you'll have material already divided into chapter topics.

## Over the long haul

Blogs evolve, and priorities change. It's impossible to draw up a road map for the future, but here are some strategic ideas to help give your blog long-term direction:

- **Write an *anchor* post every month or two.** An anchor post is a tutorial-style piece that teaches your readers how to do something, like *How to Pick Fruit at its Peak of Flavor* or *Top 10 Ways to Prevent Identity Theft*. It can be the length of a short magazine article, perhaps 750 to 1,500 words. This type of content is evergreen—it won't become obsolete, and you can continually refer back to it in your subsequent posts. Every month or two, add another anchor post.

- **Write at least one new post a day.** Frequent posting keeps your audience interested and jogs your creativity. The more you post, the more you'll be picked up by the search engines, and the more new people will find your blog, become regular readers and buy your book. The first two sentences are the hardest of a post, and it's all downhill after that.

- **Comment on other blogs in your niche.** This will attract fellow bloggers and their readers who follow the link in your comment back to your blog. Make a meaningful comment that advances the discussion, don't just say "I agree."

- **Link to other blogs from within your blog posts.** With certain blogging software, this is known as a *trackback*, and leaves a summary of your blog post on the original blog. Result: More bloggers and readers find you.

- **Ask for comments on your blog.** End your posts with a question, prompting your readers for feedback. When practical, end your posts with a question like, "What do you think?", or "What's your take on this?" Readers are often more interested in what *they* have to say than in what *you* have to say.

- **Don't write when you're angry.** If you're upset, cool off for a few hours—or a day—before posting something nasty that you might regret later. It's nearly impossible to delete stuff on the Web. You might erase something from your blog, but the text can be archived in dozens of other places.

- **Link to your old content.** After you've been blogging for a while, you'll have five or six previous blog posts that were most popular with readers—drawing lots of links, traffic, and comments. For the benefit of new readers, link to these previous posts when you write about the same topics in the future. Add a small menu of these posts on the sidebar of your blog, with a heading such as **Lively Conversations** or **Greatest Hits**.

- **Add artwork.** Sprinkling stock photos and illustrations in your blog posts is a simple way to add visual appeal. Images are eyeball magnets. Writing a post about how to fix a flat tire? Include a small stock photo of someone installing a tire. The site **www.sxc.hu** has thousands of royalty-free photos you can search by keyword. You needn't illustrate your posts literally, which can get boring. Let's imagine your post concerns some type of *manipulation*. It's the key idea and the main word in your post title. How could you illustrate it? Just search for "manipulation" at the photo site mentioned above, and you'll see dozens of images you could use as a smart illustration—like photos of puppets, marionettes or chess pawns. If your first keyword doesn't find results, try a synonym—or if you're feeling ironic, try an antonym.

- **Create an RSS or Atom feed.** Be sure your blog automatically posts a feed, so readers who use an aggregator like Bloglines can read this way if they wish. You may have to turn this function on yourself, so consult your blogging service's help files.

- **Optimize your blog.** Make sure your blog "pings" the blog aggregators such as Technorati and Bloglines each time you've posted to your blog. That way your new content will be indexed immediately.

An easy way to automate this is to open a free account at **www.Feedburner.com** and enable its free Pingshot feature.

More blogging fine points:

- Write in the first person. Never talk about yourself as a different being.
- Write keyword-rich headlines. Give people a reason to start reading.
- Hook your audience in the first sentence. Ask a question or pose a challenge.
- Don't get too preachy. Blog communication isn't top-down, it's a conversation.
- Focus on *you*, *we*, and *us*.
- Don't change your blog's domain address; it's easy to lose your audience this way.
- Tell the truth.
- Read lots of blogs.
- Link liberally to other blogs. Your post can include an excerpt from the other blog in quotation marks, but don't include more than a paragraph or two—more than that could get you accused of copyright violation.
- Link to your previous posts.
- Don't be boring. Break some crockery. A good blog takes sides.
- Don't rant on side issues outside your blog's focus. Your audience will tire of this quickly.
- Break news.

- Be authentic.
- Tell stories. Have a conversation.
- Vary your sentence length. Frequently.

## Selecting your blog publishing tool

Most bloggers don't have special blogging software installed on their PC, but work on their blog from within a Web browser. Here are the most popular blogging services:

- **Blogger.com.** Owned by Google since 2003. It's free and easy. There's an add-on program enabling you to post to your blog from Microsoft Word. You can use Blogger's free Web space, Blogspot.com, but it's best to keep your content on a domain you control, like YourBookTitle.com. Do this by using Blogger's FTP feature. For instructions: **Help.Blogger.com/bin/topic.py?topic=8917.** Other blogging systems have similar options: You can publish free on their Web space, or publish on your own domain.

- **TypePad.com.** TypePad is a flexible and professional-looking platform, but takes a bit longer to learn than Blogger. Still, you'll have many options for personalizing your blog without having to learn HTML computer code. Basic service costs $4.95 a month; the Plus level costs $8.95 a month and gives you up to three blogs hosted on your own domain. A 30-day free trial is available.

## Advertising-supported blogs

A free account at an advertising-subsidized site is another option, but you'll have less control over the design, and the advertising can distract readers:

- **spaces.live.com.** Microsoft offers the Spaces service as part of its Live suite of online services. You can produce a blog that contains small advertisements, or pay a fee to turn off the ads.

- **360.Yahoo.com.** Yahoo offers its 360 blogs, another free ad-supported service.

- **MySpace.com.** A blog is part of the package for users who set up a free MySpace profile, which is ad-supported. Similar free services are provided on the many other social-networking sites, but MySpace is the most popular. More on that later.

## Blog-to-e-mail service

Loyal readership is key to your blog's success, so make it easy for first-time visitors to keep reading. One of the simplest ways for readers to receive your blog posts is by e-mail subscription.

FeedBlitz.com and Feedburner.com operate two popular, free blog-to-e-mail services. Both provide a snippet of code you can insert on your blog to display a sign-up box or button where readers can provide their e-mail address. Subscribers receive an e-mail digest of any new blog posts, and can click through to your site to read more.

A subscription service makes it more likely that readers will stay with you because they won't need to remember to return to your Web site. An e-mail service is a simple solution for your readers who might not understand how to use Bloglines or other newsreaders.

Only about 20 percent of blog readers understand newsreaders, "so if you're not using e-mail, you're missing 80 percent of your potential audience," says Phil Hollows, chief executive of FeedBlitz.

FeedBlitz's free service also includes some reporting tools showing how many of your e-mails are opened and which of your post headlines readers click most. Knowing which of your posts gets the biggest response is a valuable insight, showing you what content readers value most.

Some authors and publishers who used to publish monthly e-mail newsletters have abandoned their newsletters and now deliver similar content in smaller, more frequent chunks using blog-to-e-mail.

E-mail service also provides you with a valuable business asset. You'll have access to those readers directly, so you can send special messages for events like publication dates and book tours. This is why many bloggers encourage readers to sign up for e-mail delivery: It provides an automatic marketing channel for special messages about you and your book, without having to manually collect contact information by some other means.

The blog-to-e-mail services provide a fully automated double opt-in process, so there's no danger of your blog posts or occasional promotional messages being mistaken for spam.

## Profiles

Blogging systems such as Google's Blogger make it simple for you to post a Profile page, where you can enter a photograph, short biography, and additional contact information. If you think your photo will not damage your book sales, you should include it on your blog. Your readers will feel a firmer connection if they can see your photo.

With the right details added, profiles can serve as a makeshift "press room" until you have one ready. Authors who already have books on the market sometimes use their Amazon profile as the profile for their personal blogs.

# Author blog platforms up close

An author with a popular blog has a valuable platform, a way of cutting through the noise and clutter. It's a direct channel to your audience, the same kind of asset that enables network TV news anchors to write bestselling memoirs.

Blogs aren't magic, though. They can't make a losing book into a winner. Plenty of blog-based books have flopped because the publishers mistakenly believed a blog audience would automatically translate into demand for a weak book.

Some publishers remain skeptical of blogs as a vehicle for book promotion. Frequent questions are:

- Who would buy a book when they can read it for free?
- Will blogging distract the author from writing a good book?
- Could the blog exhaust interest in the book before it's available?

The reality is, online content makes it much easier for the audience to discover a book and develop an appetite for it. Is it possible for a single author to promote a single title using a simple blog? Many who have done it well have had tremendous success:

## Business

**www.LongTail.com.** *The Long Tail*, a bestselling 2006 business book, originated with a Wired magazine article that grew into a blog. The *Long Tail* idea is that niche products are becoming increasingly important, and someday the niches might account for more aggregate sales than the occasional blockbuster books, movies, and other products.

The magazine article drew a huge reaction, so author Chris Anderson continued his research as an "open source" experiment in book development. He shared his latest ideas with blog readers, who responded with more ideas, tested his analysis, and lead him in new directions. The blog's readership grew among a cross section of publishing, retailing and technology enthusiasts, assembling a built-in audience for the book.

Even as his 2006 book tour took him to Europe and back, Anderson continued updating the blog, where the Long Tail conversation continues today.

## Humor

**www.TheBestPageInTheUniverse.com.** A great example of the word-of-mouth power of blogs is *Alphabet of Manliness*, a satire book by first-time author George Ouzounian.

Like most "overnight successes," this one actually resulted from years of steady craftsmanship. With no professional writing credentials or audience, Ouzounian began posting a sexist, profane, politically incorrect Web site using the pseudonym Maddox. By 2006, his daily readership reached 150,000, and a specialty publisher persuaded him to compile the blog material into a book.

When his book was ready, Ouzounian needed only to press a button to create a No. 1 bestseller on Amazon: sending an e-mail to his registered readers, telling them his book was for sale.

Maddox is one of several young amateur comedy writers who've struck gold in book publishing after proving their material on a blog. Other recent bestsellers include *Real Ultimate Power: The Official Ninja Book*, by Robert Hamburger (a pseudonym), *I Hope They Serve Beer in Hell* by Tucker Max, and *The Modern Drunkard* by Frank Kelly Rich.

Some of the humor bloggers try to appear as adolescent and rude as possible. For example, Hamburger's book description on Amazon begins this way:

> Dear Stupid Idiots,
>
> A lot of you have been saying that I don't know anything about REAL ninjas. But that's a bunch of bull crap! You dummies don't know anything. And maybe YOU should get a life. I bet a lot of you have never even seen a girl naked!

**www.TimBete.com.** Here's a humor blog for grown-ups. Tim Bete uses this site to publish his award-winning parenting humor column, previously featured in the *Christian Science Monitor* and several parenting magazines. He used the blog as a launch pad for his 2005 book *In the Beginning ... There Were No Diapers*.

## Politics

**www.glenngreenwald.blogspot.com.** Passions run high on political blogs, and the field is a rich training ground for authors. Glenn Greenwald, a constitutional law attorney who started the blog *Unclaimed Territory* in 2005, was recruited just eight months later to write *How Would a Patriot Act?* Thanks to exposure on Greenwald's blog and seven others, the book made it to Amazon's No. 1 spot and the New York Times bestseller list before it was even in print. Like many blog-to-book successes, this one was grass-roots—it wasn't promoted in review publications like *Publishers Weekly* or *Kirkus Reviews* and was ignored by mainstream print and television media.

Greenwald went from rookie blogger to bestselling author in six months.

## Arts and crafts

**www.52Projects.com.** Arts and crafts are a natural for bloggers with a knack for teaching. Author Jeff Yamaguchi, publisher of the popular crafts blog *52Projects*, translated the success of his blog into a spin-off book, *52 Projects: Random Acts of Everyday Creativity*, published by Perigee. The book's success fueled further traffic to his blog, and spawned an online community.

## Diaries

**www.Wilwheaton.typepad.com.** Wil Wheaton is a former child star best known for his role in the 1986 film *Stand By Me* and his boyhood run on *Star Trek: The Next Generation*. After a 1990s lull, Wheaton re-invented his career by blogging, then self-publishing. His first book, *Dancing Barefoot*, expanded on his autobiographical blog posts. After it quickly sold 3,000 copies, Wheaton signed a three-book deal with O'Reilly & Associates Inc., the computer book publisher.

**www.CBftw.blogspot.com** Another popular book drawn from blog posts of a young amateur writer is *My War: Killing Time in Iraq*. The blog by Colby Buzzell, a 28-year-old Army machine gun "trigger puller" stationed in Iraq's notorious Sunni Triangle, got so popular that his Army commander pulled the plug. But Buzzell continued writing, and Putnam published an acclaimed book based on the blog in October 2005.

## Romance

**www.BillBranley.com.** Bill Branley, a writer and jazz musician from New Orleans, first wrote *Sea Changes* as a blog, then self-published it as a book. Reader response was so strong that he acquired an agent to shop the story to major publishers and movie studios. Branley has another blog devoted to his unpublished story *Night Watch* at **www.FerryTale.blogspot.com**.

Branley also wrote *Peggy Finds a Friend*, a fiction blog published in 2005. See archives: **www.BillBranley.com/pictures.html**.

## Memoir

**www.Poundy.com.** Children's book editor Wendy McClure started an online journal about her new diet. Her blog, Poundy.com, expanded on her thoughts about body-image psychology. A few years later, the blog became a popular memoir, *I'm Not the New Me*. McClure followed up in 2006 with *The Amazing Mackerel Pudding Plan*.

An avid photographer, McClure also posts to Flickr.com to share photos with her readers and friends. During book tours, she posts pictures of her stops and local scenery. McClure links to the Flickr page from her book's Web page so she can provide fans with fresh content, even when there isn't time for writing new blog posts.

**www.Jennsylvania.com.** This intimate yet irreverent blog spawned the memoir *Bitter is the New Black* by Jen Lancaster.

**www.Pamie.com.** Pamela Ribon hit the Amazon Top 200 in fiction after turning this dark, funny online diary into a 2003 novel, *Why Girls Are Weird*. She followed up in 2006 with *Why Moms Are Weird*.

# Mystery

**www.Hackoff.com**. Tom Evslin, a former executive with Microsoft and AT&T, started this blog to serialize his first book, *hackoff.com: An Historic Murder Mystery Set in the Internet Bubble and Rubble*. Each passage from the book was published on the blog as Evslin wrote it, automatically building an audience for the book. He self-published the story in 2006 as a 642-page hardcover, supporting it with a book tour and Amazon Connect blog, where he publicized each tour appearance.

Evslin also has the entire text of the book posted for free viewing on his site in the format of a *blook*, a term combining book and blog. To aid readability, blooks are presented in chronological order, as opposed to a blog, which presents material in reverse chronological order—most recent on top. While Evslin's blook is designed to be read online, other authors have used the term blook to describe printed books composed mainly of blog posts.

You can read Evslin's book on the site or subscribe to daily episodes delivered via e-mail or an RSS feed. You can also listen to free audio podcasts of him reading each section.

Evslin also publishes a popular technology blog, *Fractals of Change*, **http://blog.tomevslin.com**, which helps funnel traffic to his book blog.

**www.DailyPundit.com.** Longtime fiction writer William Quick used his popular political blog as a launch platform for a self-published novel. After five years of trying to sell his conspiracy novel *Inner Circles* to a trade publisher, Quick posted it on his blog in e-book form in September 2005. Within weeks, he sold more than 900 copies at $5 apiece, raking in $4,500. Blog visitors still buy about 100 copies of the book per month.

Since releasing his e-book, Quick has also begun selling hard copies. The 329-page paperback costs $17.95.

# Publishing

**www.MJRoseblog.typepad.com.** You'd think M.J. Rose would be busy enough writing her bestselling novels, but she also publishes two popular blogs aimed at writers. *Backstory* features guest columns by novelists who want to share the "secrets, truths, and logical and illogical moments that sparked their fiction." Contributors send in an essay of 500 to 900 words along with their author photo and cover art.

Rose's other blog is *Buzz, Balls and Hype*, which features current articles about book marketing:

**www.mjroseblog.typepad.com/buzz_balls_hype**

**www.FonerBooks.com/cornered.htm.** Morris Rosenthal got started in self-publishing in the 1990s by posting some ideas for a computer book on his Web site. Word spread quickly, and by simply answering one question from a reader each day, Rosenthal attracted a big following and sales of his book took off. That led to this blog and a related book about self-publishing, *Print-On-Demand Book Publishing*.

**www.JWikert.typepad.com.** Joe Wikert is executive publisher in the professional/trade division of John Wiley & Sons. His *Publishing 2020* blog provides daily commentary on new-media issues, and dispenses the kind of advice that's hard to find, such as how big an advance authors can expect, whether you need an agent, and how to know who the good ones are.

## Blogs into blooks

It's getting more common for authors to blog their book as they write it, or condense the contents of a blog into a book, or *blook*. **www.Blogbasedbooks.com** and **www.Blurb.com** offer free software like BookSmart, which automatically converts a blog or MySpace site into a book by deleting the hyperlinks, time-stamps and other Web formatting. But the prices aren't competitive with regular offset or on-demand book printing; Blurb charges $29.99 for a 40-page hardcover. Mostly these services attract vanity projects, where authors are willing to pay a premium to avoid the tasks of book layout and design.

# Blog tours

So far, we've explored techniques for luring readers to your blog or Web site. Now we'll turn to outreach campaigns—going where part of your potential readership already congregates.

You can introduce your book to lots more readers with a series of appearances on blogs catering to your audience—a *blog tour*. Sometimes it's called *guest blogging* or a *virtual book tour*.

Blog tours are especially valuable for authors unable to travel, uncomfortable with public speaking, or whose dispersed audience makes touring impractical. Blog tours can expose your book to a much larger audience than a traditional bookstore tour, while requiring less time and money. Blog tours are especially helpful in launching new books.

"Blogs are like rocket fuel for online book publicity," said Steve O'Keefe, executive director of Patron Saint Productions, a book publicity firm.

Blog tours are also a good deal for the host blogger, who gets free content for his or her readers and affiliate revenue from book sales.

Typical blog tours include these elements:

- An **excerpt** displayed on the host blog to publicize the tour appearance.

- A one-day **appearance**, beginning with an opening statement, a short essay on the topic of your book. Then the floor is open for discussion.

- **Follow-up visits** for the next four to seven days to answer questions and comments from blog readers.

## Targeting host blogs

Your first step in arranging a blog tour is finding potential host blogs. Find the most popular blogs read by your book's target audience.

Some likely candidates may spring to mind, but new blogs can gain readership quickly, so it's worth surveying the field periodically.

Building your list of target blogs requires some legwork because there is no current, comprehensive directory of all blogs. To determine the popularity, authority, and quality of blogs in your niche, you'll need to sample the content yourself.

Start your search here:

- **www.Technorati.com.** This blog tracking site lists the top 100 most popular blogs at **Technorati.com/pop/blogs**. But to find niche content, you'll need to look beyond these mainstream blogs. Consult the advanced search tool, **Technorati.com/search**, where you can drill down into specific topics.

- **www.Blogsearch.Google.com.** Type in keywords related to your book. Ignore results from personal blogs that focus on the author and get little traffic.

- **www.Forbes.com/bow/b2c/main.jhtml.** Forbes' "Best of the Web" directory reviews blogs with high-quality content.

Once you've identified a list of potential blog hosts, prioritize them by three criteria: activity level, reader involvement and traffic volume.

- **Activity level.** How frequently do new posts appear on the blog? Bloggers usually must post new content a few times week to sustain a loyal readership. Scan the past few months of blog archives to determine the posting frequency.

- **Reader involvement.** How often do readers chime in with thoughtful comments? The vast majority of blogs allow readers to follow up with their own commentary. The frequency and thoughtfulness of reader comments indicates audience engagement.

- **Traffic volume.** Traffic is the natural result of audience loyalty and involvement, and it's an objective measure of a blog's impact. A handy yardstick for measuring blog traffic is **www.Alexa.com**, which provides estimated traffic reports on many Web sites.

At Alexa.com, click Traffic Rankings at the top navigation bar. Enter the address of the blog you want to evaluate and click Get Traffic Details. For most blogs, you'll see an Alexa rank from 1 (the most-visited site on the Web) to about 5 million, meaning very low readership. For the top 100,000 sites, Alexa provides detailed traffic estimates. Under the heading **Explore this site**, you'll see these links:

- Traffic Details shows the blog's relative reach and number of page views, and whether traffic is trending up or down.

- Related Links shows other sites popular with the same audience. Here you can discover more blogs frequented by your target audience.

- Sites Linking In shows which sites, ranked by authority, have incoming links to the blog. Follow these links, and you'll find more sites targeting your audience.

Depending on how narrowly focused your book is, you may find only a few relevant quality blogs, and that's fine. It's better to focus on a small, well-qualified audience who will respond to your book instead of a general audience where you'll have little impact.

Alexa's reports aren't foolproof; they're drawn from a small sample of Web users who use its browser toolbar. Rankings for high-traffic sites are more statistically accurate than reports for niche sites. In any case, Alexa is a handy, free source of objective information about Web traffic, and is more accurate than anecdotal reports. Bloggers and Webmasters are notorious for overestimating their traffic.

Alexa, which is a subsidiary of Amazon.com, isn't limited to blogs, so you can use it to find all sorts of Web sites targeting your niche. Another good source of traffic estimates is **www.MetricsMarket.com**.

## Google PageRank

Another way of determining how much juice a blog has is Google PageRank. It's a patented method Google uses to rank the importance of Web sites on a scale of one to 10 based on the authority of incoming links. Google offers a free toolbar you can use to check rankings:

**http://toolbar.google.com**

Quality blogs and Web sites will have a PageRank of at least five. To determine PageRank, check the blog's main page or a Web site's home page; other pages often are unranked.

## Building your excerpt

Now that you've identified where you'd like to appear on your blog tour, the next step is creating your excerpt. The excerpt is an online document providing a description of the book, a passage from the text, cover artwork, and an author photo and biography. Your excerpt can resemble a traditional paper book flier but include more detail.

Your excerpt serves three purposes:

- To convince the blogger to host your appearance.
- To promote your appearance to the blog's readers.
- To prepare the blog audience to discuss issues and ideas raised in your book.

Essential information like the author name and book title should be embedded and visible on the photos of the cover art and author photo. That way, if a Webmaster accidentally leaves out part of your text—or it's deleted at some point—readers will still have enough information to buy your book. If possible, combine all the elements of your excerpt into a single document to ensure it's displayed properly and nothing is omitted.

A typical excerpt includes these elements:

- A brief setup to the book, describing its topic, audience, and perspective.
- Title, author name and retail price.
- Blurbs and testimonials.
- Credentials of nonfiction authors.
- A short excerpt from the book.
- Affiliate links to buy the book at online retailers.
- Author photo.
- Other bibliographic information such as ISBN, binding, page count, and publisher.

Try to cap your excerpt at 2,000 to 3,000 words. Some readers won't persist in scrolling down two screens of continuous content.

However, interested readers often print longer excerpts, so you should include a message encouraging printing at the top of long excerpts.

## Excerpts that sell

Imagine you're riding in an elevator with a potential reader of your book. You have 20 seconds before the elevator door opens and your companion leaves. What can you say to compel him or her to walk to the nearest bookstore and buy your book as soon as the door opens? The answer is the heart of your excerpt.

When selecting sample passages, don't automatically take your excerpt from the front of the book. Material from a book's introduction can be dull for an unfamiliar audience.

More hints for a compelling excerpt:

- **Give chunks, not boulders.** For nonfiction, make your excerpt *the most essential, engaging* nuggets in your book. Winning excerpts often contain lists, like "Top 10 ways to save money when buying a car" or "Three ways to ask someone on a date."

- **Cliffhangers.** For fiction, try leaving readers in midair. Encourage interest in one or two characters.

- **News angle.** For either fiction or nonfiction, try to find a news hook. Is there a current controversy or movie related to your book's topic? Topicality is blog oxygen. For fiction and nonfiction, a strong current-events hook can persuade A-list bloggers to host your tour.

- **Benefits, not features.** For nonfiction, briefly describe the benefits—what problems does it solve? Explain how your book differs from competing titles. If you've received a truly impressive blurb or endorsement, include it.

- **White space.** Break up your text. Separate paragraphs with blank lines, inserting some white space between the gray blocks of text. Readers are more likely to read your excerpt if they can scan chunks of text.

- **All together now.** If your excerpt is accompanied by more than one image, assemble everything in a layout file in PDF or HTML format.

This prevents the blogger or Webmaster from losing a piece of your excerpt.

Don't send your excerpt as an e-mail attachment. Most people are apprehensive of receiving files from unfamiliar people. Instead, post the document on a dedicated page on your domain, and provide the link. Then your hosts can copy the document or link to it. After you've posted the file on your domain, don't delete it, because some blogs will link to your page instead of keeping the material on their site. The excerpt on your domain may get traffic for years to come.

To see an example of an excerpt, see:

**www.PatronSaintPr.com/samples/mclaren/mclaren-obd.htm**

In this excerpt, the title and author name is followed by an "Introduction" briefly establishing the author's credentials and describing the book. Next comes a passage from the text, more information about the book, bibliographic details, and a link to the publisher's Web site.

If you're working under contract with a publisher, ensure you're authorized to distribute excerpts. Many authors are surprised to learn they don't have online rights to their work. If necessary, get written permission in an e-mail from your publisher's marketing department. Often publishers will provide a PDF for your use as an online excerpt.

## Your pitch to bloggers

Now your excerpt is ready and you've compiled a list of blogs for your tour. It's time to pitch your tour to the host bloggers. Contact each blogger individually by e-mail, explaining why your book is of interest.

Provide two or three compelling reasons why your tour will be thought-provoking and entertaining for *this blog's audience.*

Start with your top prospects and work your way down as time permits. Contact bloggers directly; don't simply leave a comment on their blog and hope they notice it. Most blogs have a mechanism for contacting the blogger through an e-mail address or contact form.

Sometimes the more popular a blogger is, the harder it is to get their attention. If you can't find contact information, look at the bottom of the home page, where you may see instructions for contacting the "Webmaster." Sometimes an "advertise with us" link is the most reliable way of reaching a decision-maker.

Tailor your pitch for each blogger, addressing them by name, otherwise your message can be mistaken for spam. Offer a complimentary review copy of your book. Provide your complete contact information including phone number, which also differentiates your message from spam. The subject line of your e-mail must be specific; a generic "Please read this" often is deleted unread.

The excerpt includes everything the blogger needs to decide whether to approve your tour appearance. If approved, a copy of the excerpt can be posted at the host blog to promote your appearance in the days preceding the tour. Schedule no more than three to five blogs per week, which should keep you busy.

## A sample pitch

Here's a sample script for pitching your blog tour:

> SUBJECT: Author [NAME] as guest on [BLOG NAME]
>
> Dear [BLOGGER NAME]
>
> I'm a regular reader of your blog, and believe it's one of the best sites about [TOPIC]. I'm writing to see if you would consider having me as a guest on your blog on Monday, May 9, to discuss my book [TITLE].
>
> I believe my book is of particular interest to your readership. [REASONS, BRIEFLY]

> I'm hoping to have a dialog with your readers. If you approve, I'll take a day on your blog, make an opening statement, and respond to comments as long as they keep coming.
>
> I hope you'll give this a try. I've prepared an HTML document with a short excerpt from the book and its cover art. You can view the document here at my site: http://www.example.com. You're free to reproduce this document on your site or provide links.
>
> I'd also like to send a complimentary review copy of the book, just let me know where to mail it.
>
> Thanks for your consideration,
> [SIGNATURE]
> [POSTAL ADDRESS]
> [PHONE NUMBER]

Not every blogger will accept your pitch, and you shouldn't take the rejections personally—an acceptance rate of 25 percent is a good target. Some sites simply don't use book excerpts. Often blogs run by newspapers or magazines don't use third-party content except in sections labeled "opinion" or "to the editor."

As realistically as possible, pitch yourself as a potential long-term partner, not a drive-by opportunist. Successful blog tours will prompt return invitations and can launch a mutually beneficial relationship.

## Your guest appearance

On the day of your blog tour appearance, open with a short statement, recapping the themes expressed in your book excerpt, and ask the blog audience for its reaction. Depending on how the blogger administers the site, you may be given a login and password for the site, or simply e-mail your material to the blogger.

Reaction from the blog audience can continue for several days, giving you the opportunity to reappear, replying to comments and answering questions.

# Blog conversation

When responding to a blog audience, be succinct and keep the conversation moving. Blog conversation is a two-way street, and exchanging ideas makes compelling content. At the end of each of your responses, conclude with a question, such as "What's your take on that?" or "How do you feel about this?"

Be prepared for the occasional rude or embarrassing question. For example, if your book is about barbecuing, be ready for questions from animal-rights activists. Feel free to ignore off-topic comments, and simply continue with your message. But don't shy away from substantive arguments—nothing sells a book better than controversy.

At each stop on your blog tour, mention your previous appearances on other blogs and provide the links. This will generate continued readership and cross-linking among blogs.

# Archiving your results

Keeping screen shots of your blog appearances and a journal of your correspondence with bloggers can come in handy later. You can review the tour to see which sites and techniques were effective. Record the contact information for each blogger: their e-mail addresses, phone numbers, and mailing addresses. This way you'll have a running start if you decide to conduct another blog tour some months later.

To see archived screen shots of a blog tour, see:

**www.PatronSaintPr.com/samples/mclaren/mclaren-blogreport.htm**

# Encore appearances

Blog tours don't always cause a big spike in sales, but they do fuel word of mouth for your book and build name recognition. Each time you appear in front of your target audience, it's a plus. When a blog appearance goes particularly well, don't let it end there. Offer to write a monthly guest column for the blog in exchange for a link to your site and a permanent buy-the-book affiliate link.

Map out your blog tour strategy a few months before your publication date. But don't make the mistake of scheduling a blog tour or any other publicity before your book is available for sale. Blog tours spark impulse sales, so make sure anyone who wants the book is able to buy it.

## More resources

The blog tour strategy outlined here is based on one developed by Patron Saint Productions, a literary consulting firm. For do-it-yourselfers, its Web site contains free sample materials you can adapt for your own tour:

**www.PatronSaintPR.com/samples.html**

Another literary consultancy that specializes in blog tours is Author Marketing Experts Inc., headed by author Penny Sansevieri. Her site also features several free resources and a newsletter. See:

**www.amarketingexpert.com/free.html**

# Social networking

When 24-year-old Steven Oliverez finished writing his debut fantasy novel, he faced the same predicament as most new authors. He wanted to sell the manuscript, but couldn't get a single publisher to *read it*, let alone buy it. He spent two years writing query letters, and all he got was a stack of form-letter rejections.

So Oliverez decided to self-publish and promote the book himself. Fortunately, he wasn't starting from scratch. He'd been active on the wildly popular social site MySpace, networking with other fantasy readers and authors. On his MySpace blog, he'd given away seven of his short stories to anyone willing to read them. His stories prompted hundreds of enthusiastic comments and attracted thousands of MySpace "friends."

So when Oliverez published *Elder Staves* in 2005, he asked for a little help from his MySpace friends. He asked them to buy the book on Amazon, and they did—pushing it to No. 25 on the fantasy bestseller list. Then Oliverez started getting messages from book clubs around the country, asking if he'd make phone-in appearances. After that came some write-ups in publishing trade magazines. Few tools can attract and bind an audience than a network like MySpace, Oliverez says:

> Buzz creates more buzz. Since there's no marketing or publishing company behind the book, it really helps to be online, able to connect with readers directly. Being on MySpace makes you seem more approachable, and that makes it a great tool for authors.

Next Oliverez printed 30,000 personalized bookmarks, and asked his MySpace friends to pass them out at bookstores and coffee shops. Immediately he got a few dozen volunteers. Then Oliverez found more MySpace friends by joining several of its "groups" for authors and fiction-writing.

You can visit Oliverez on MySpace and read the first two chapters of his book at:

**www.MySpace.com/Oliverez**

## MySpace: Not just for kids

What Oliverez did wasn't new. He took a page from the thousands of unsigned rock bands that have tapped MySpace to build their audiences. It's a simple yet wonderfully effective strategy: The bands put samples of their music on their MySpace profile, and friends forward the songs to an ever-enlarging circle of friends. Bands that "go viral" on MySpace sell lots more concert tickets and CDs, and some have snagged major recording contracts. Even the journeymen are raking it in by hawking their disks, T-shirts and other goodies right on MySpace.

Authors are quickly realizing they can do the same thing the bands are doing: use MySpace to go directly to their audience, without needing a big fat marketing campaign or the muscle of a big publisher.

Barely two years after its launch, MySpace became the most popular U.S. Web site based on number of visits during 2006. Each member has his or her own circle of like-minded friends. After you become someone's MySpace friend, you have access to his or her friends. And each of your new friends has more friends.

While there are hundreds of social-networking sites—Facebook, Friendster, Orkut and Tribe.net to name just a few—MySpace has captured more than 80 percent of the traffic. If you want to see what all the fuss is about, you can open a MySpace account here:

**www.Signup.Myspace.com/index.cfm?fuseaction=join**

If you wish, you can make your MySpace account private until you're ready to use it. Go to **Account Settings** and then **Privacy Settings**.

MySpace? You might be thinking, "Isn't that for high-school kids?" Sure, that's the stereotype; MySpace is popular with kids. But with nearly 100 million members and the No. 1 traffic rank on the entire Internet, clearly there's more to it than loitering schoolkids.

Authors of every genre are jumping on the MySpace bandwagon. Horror novelist Michael Laimo says he got more than a dozen big media interviews after reporters noticed his MySpace page. He inked his first movie deal through MySpace after an independent director sent him a MySpace message asking about film rights. Hundreds of fans have told him they bought his books after seeing his MySpace profile:

**www.MySpace.com/MichaelLaimo**

MySpace is the Internet's answer to a promotional tactic used by new authors for decades—selling books from the trunk of your car. Both tactics are tedious, time-consuming, and usually don't produce results for a while. But if you keep plugging away and you're sincere, people notice. Your snowball starts barreling downhill purely from its own momentum.

Here are some of the friends you can network with on MySpace:

- **Readers.** People who read similar kinds of books, on the same topics and in the same genres. People who read the same authors as you, or whose style you emulate. You can search for these readers using any keywords or names related to your themes and books.

- **Authors.** Other authors are great people to network with—creative types in the same boat as you, trying to find new readers. You'll find many valuable ways to share resources and cross-promote with authors you meet on MySpace.

- **Agents and publishers.** Book publishers want to find authors who already have a following, a platform that can be turned into readership and book buyers. One obvious way of showing you can do it is making a name for yourself on MySpace.

Most of its members don't use MySpace as a promotion tool; they're just there for the friends. But MySpace can be a foolproof self-promotional tool if you're intent on using it that way. Any author, even one without computer skills, can easily post photos along with artwork and sample text from their books. You can include links to buy your book from online retailers, publish a MySpace blog, and send bulletins about your public appearances and publication dates.

Big publishers have noticed the potential for publicity on MySpace too, and have been building profiles for their authors, often using the same canned material from press releases. Readers who are already fans might be interested in this warmed-over stuff, but authors building an audience must get involved. You can't fake participation online for very long.

In addition to its networking opportunities, MySpace is a wickedly good research tool. For example, in about 10 seconds you can find out how many members say "Malcolm Gladwell" is their favorite author, and you can zap a message to them if you like. Or you can quickly locate members in your ZIP code who are science-fiction buffs. Authors can even use MySpace to figure out what books their own friends and fans are currently reading.

## Making friends on MySpace

There are several ways to find people on MySpace who might be in your target audience—by searching for *murder mysteries*, *historical romance*, *self-improvement*, *organic food*, or whatever field you're in. Perhaps there's a famous writer whose style you emulate, and you'd like to find other admirers. Once you've found potential friends, you can send a request for them to "add" you as a friend. The invitee can accept, decline, or ignore your request, although most people accept.

Once you're friends with someone on MySpace, you can post comments on each other's profile pages and see each other's full circle of friends. Here's how to find friends and potential readership on MySpace:

- **Browse friends lists of similar authors.** Find the MySpace profiles of authors with similar books, writing style, and similar target audience as yours. On the right side, scroll down a bit to the link See All of [Name]'s Friends. Start sending invitations—you'll get many potential readers this way. For example, up-and-coming memoirist Josh Kilmer-Purcell sends friend invitations to fans of David Sedaris and Augustine Burroughs, bestselling memoirists in the same vein. Each time he makes his rounds on MySpace, Purcell watches his Amazon sales spike for days afterward. Here's another twist: Send a friend invitation to a famous author, and if they accept, post a comment, which appears on the bottom right of their MySpace page. More exposure for you.

- **Search.** Click Search on the top toolbar on the MySpace home page. You can limit your search to certain areas such as Books Interest, Blogs, Music Interest, or others. Let's imagine you're looking for MySpace members interested in organic food. Click on Search, Book Interest, and enter "organic food." Presto, you've got a list of every MySpace member who's used the words "organic food" in their profile. Use the same search technique to find subjects, genres, and author names. Also, use the **Affiliations for Networking** search tool a bit farther down the page. You can search the fields "Marketing" or "Publishing" using your keywords to find potential MySpace friends who could share book-marketing resources and tips.

- **Browsing for friends.** If you have a travel book or title of regional interest, it might be useful to browse for potential MySpace friends by geographic area. On the home page, click Browse and the **Advanced** tab. You'll be able to view member profiles within a specified distance of Postal Service ZIP codes, as well as other criteria such as age, gender, religion, and income. Many single MySpace members use this function to scout potential dates, but it can be useful for entrepreneurs as well.

- **Browse comments on other authors' profiles.** Comments from MySpace friends appear on the bottom right of profile pages. The most recent comments appear at the top, accompanied by the comment writer's photo or image. Members who leave these comments tend to be the most active and vocal MySpace users, and make good friends. In particular, seek out people who've posted thoughtful comments, like "Enjoyed seeing your profile and can't wait to read the next book." Skip messages such as, "You ROCK, Man!!!"

**Sending friends requests.** Once you find a potential friend, click Add to Friends under their main photo on the left. And if you want to increase the odds of making a real connection, don't stop there—send a personalized message by clicking the Send a Message link. It requires some extra work, but you can't convert people into book buyers simply by pecking on your mouse button.

**Accepting friends.** Once you've done some networking on MySpace, people will start seeking you out. But don't feel obligated to accept anyone and everyone. Click to their profile page first, and make sure their interests are in line with yours.

There are two ways of approaching MySpace friendships: trying to acquire as big a list as possible, or having a smaller group you can make stronger connections with individually. In any case, the people who ultimately buy your books and recommend you to others will be those in your core groups, those who feel a connection.

**Leaving comments.** After you become someone's MySpace friend, visit their profile and add a comment. This is an effective networking tool—not only will your new friend read your comment, but people who visit your friend's page will see it too. Avoid the most overused MySpace comment: "Thanks for the add," which means "thanks for adding me as a friend." It's a cliché, and a missed opportunity. Take a moment to think of a meaningful comment, based on something about your new friend's profile, like "Hey, my favorite author is Hemingway too!"

**Sending messages.** MySpace has an internal e-mail system and an instant-messaging system for sending private notes. You can include your regular e-mail signature, including links and photos. But if the message isn't too personal, you're better off posting your thoughts publicly, as a "comment" on your friend's page. This increases your visibility on MySpace, making it that much easier for new friends and readers to discover you.

**Responding to messages.** When you receive a MySpace message, you'll receive an e-mail alert. To network effectively, respond promptly to your messages. If someone makes the effort to write to you, they'll be waiting for a response. Don't alienate potential friends by letting messages pile up unanswered.

Sending personal replies is time-consuming and you won't see instant results. But remember, the personal connection you provide with a thoughtful reply is something readers will remember, and something they're unlikely to get from a big-name author. These are the folks who will feel good about you and recommend your books to others.

**Sending bulletins.** Once you've built a network of MySpace friends, the ability to send MySpace bulletins is a powerful tool. Your message won't be e-mailed like your personal messages are, but its headline will appear on all your friends' home pages in the box labeled My Bulletin Space. Whether you have two dozen MySpace friends or 20,000, the ability to let them all know about your new book at the same time is a unique tool.

To post a bulletin, click the Post bulletin link in the box labeled **My Mail**.

Like personal messages, bulletins are a feature you'll want to use sparingly, to preserve their impact. If you bombard friends with frequent bulletins that aren't compelling, they'll start ignoring them, and perhaps be irritated enough to drop you as a friend.

Here are the kinds of noteworthy events you'll want to send bulletins about:

- Your new book becomes available for sale at online retailers or local bookstores.
- You get profiled in a national newspaper or magazine.
- You've won a prestigious award or literary prize.
- You've just been booked to appear on *The Oprah Winfrey Show* or *Larry King Live*.

## Picking your 'Top 8'

After you've explored MySpace a bit, you'll notice under each member's **About Me** section are pictures of eight friends, along with a link to that member's complete friends list. By default, the eight pictures displayed are the first eight friends added by that member, known in MySpace parlance as the Top 8.

You can shuffle your Top 8 to add zing to your profile page. Take your most influential or well-known friends and move them to the front by scrolling down to the box labeled **My Friend Space** and clicking Change my Top Friends. Seek out more authors or experts in your field, and request they add you as a friend. Move them into your Top 8 too. This is a valuable cross-promotion tool because it boosts your exposure among readers in your target audience.

If you're really popular on MySpace, don't limit yourself to just eight top friends. Click Change my Top Friends, and on the top left corner of the screen you'll see a drop-down menu where you can increase the number of Top Friends displayed on your main page to as many as 24. If you'd rather display fewer Top Friends, you can reduce it to four.

Author Marcy Dermansky creatively used her MySpace Top 8 to help promote her debut novel *Twins*. Drawing from her 3,000 MySpace friends, Dermansky found several with names matching the character names in her book, like Lauren, Chloe, and Smita. She moved them to her Top 8. For the more unusual names in the book, like Jürgen and Yumiko, she had to search for new friends using MySpace's search engine. New friends who got invitations were so intrigued about the book, they often bought it simply to read about namesake characters, adding to the book's buzz. See:

**www.MySpace.com/ChloeAndSue**

## Tips for working MySpace

After you've signed up at MySpace, pay special attention to these elements of your profile:

**Headline.** When you set up your MySpace account, you're able to upload a picture—perhaps your portrait or book cover—and a short message labeled your **headline**. Use this space to identify yourself: who you are, and what you write about. Use this to its maximum effect. Add your book title or a brief description of the type of books you write. You can update this section anytime to promote recent books or editions.

**About Me.** Here, list your history and your influences. HTML is allowed in this section, so include prominent links to your own Web site or blog, and buy-the-book links.

Although it isn't obvious, there are several things you can do to customize your MySpace profile, as long as you're willing to fiddle with the settings. For more information:

**www.MySpaceSupport.com**

**Photos.** Many authors use their book cover as their main photo on MySpace instead of a portrait. In any case, use professional photos and artwork when possible. Hire a real photographer or enlist a talented friend with a digital camera. Don't brand yourself an amateur by using a crummy snapshot.

## Your MySpace blog

As a MySpace member you're able to publish a blog linked to your profile. Here you can include content too lengthy for your messages or bulletins. Blog posts are searchable through MySpace and regular search engines like Google, so naturally you'll want to include plenty of information about your book.

If you're already publishing a blog on your own domain, you don't necessarily have to reinvent the wheel on your MySpace blog. Simply repurpose some earlier content from your own blog, posting it on your MySpace blog for the benefit of your new friends.

Ask your friends to "subscribe" to your blog by clicking Subscribe to this Blog while they're visiting. Then they'll receive e-mail alerts of your new posts.

To add a post to your blog, click Manage Blog from the menu just to the right of your main profile picture, then scroll down to the box labeled **My Controls** and click Post New Blog.

MySpace blogs contain a handy way to link to your book on Amazon. Just below the box named **Body**, where you enter your blog text, is a box labeled "Tell us what you're reading, viewing, or listening to." In the pull-down box, select **books**, then in the search box, enter your book's ISBN. This will add the link buy now from Amazon to the bottom of your blog post, along with an image of your book cover. You can forward the same link to your MySpace friends, who can post it on their blogs, adding to your exposure.

Contests and giveaways are reliable ways to promote your book on MySpace too; the only limit is your imagination. Offer a monthly drawing for a free copy of your book, awarded to one of your new friends. Just the act of offering a free drawing of your book will encourage others to buy it—they won't want to wait to see if they've won the contest.

## MySpace Groups

Joining various MySpace "groups" is perhaps the best way to find new friends. From MySpace.com, click Groups on the top navigation bar. On the left, you'll see a link for Search Groups, where you can search for your genre, topic area, favorite authors, etc. Join groups that reflect the type of books you write or like to read, or other topics that interest you.

Joining groups is a better way to connect with potential readers than just randomly sending friend invitations to any profile that you happen to see. Some groups allow you to post bulletins where you can mention your book. But check on this: It's important to know the group's terms of use, and you don't want to be accused of spamming the group.

**Interests.** Here's where you enter your basic likes, in categories such as books, music, movies, television, and others. Don't leave it blank. This is how many people will find you on MySpace, by searching for friends who have common interests.

## Create your own group

You can create your own MySpace group, giving members several more avenues to discover you. You can attract a wider readership by forming a group dedicated to your subgenre or topic. And by doing a good job of running the show, you'll establish your credibility as an expert in your field.

If you already have a big, dedicated following, you can make it all about you, starting a fan club Group for yourself on MySpace. Or you can enlist one of your friends to do it.

## Dedicated pages for titles, characters

Some authors create a separate MySpace profile dedicated to each new book they write, using the book title as the profile name. After creating the profile, these authors often send bulletins to all their friends, requesting that they add their new book's profile to their friends list, getting more exposure. For fiction authors, creating a MySpace profile for a fictional character can be an attention grabber.

## MySpace Books?

In 2006, MySpace created its own music-recording label following the success of many unsigned bands on its site. Creation of a book publishing subsidiary could be a logical next step.

MySpace created a special section devoted to books in 2006, which includes rankings on several hundred books by popularity—how many times the book has been linked to on Amazon by a MySpace blog.

You can find MySpace's book section by going to www.MySpace.com and clicking Books from the upper left navigation box. The area also features a "books" blog, three genre-based book groups—such as Writers Lounge, Classic Literature Lovers and Mindless Creativeness—and a list of several "featured books."

Certainly MySpace's books section will grow as the site matures. MySpace was bought in 2005 by the media conglomerate News Corp. Like Amazon, MySpace is well positioned to provide micro-publishing and vanity publishing services to its millions of members.

## Uploading videos

Video is a great way to promote yourself and your work on MySpace. People respond more when they can associate a face and a voice with the words.

Lots of new companies have popped up recently to provide authors with video content to promote their books. If you don't have the resources to hire a video producer, it's fairly easy to create your own video. A simple question-and-answer session can provide video content to publicize your book. Position yourself in a chair in front of a bookshelf or potted plant and have a friend ask a series of questions about you, your book, who it's written for, and why you wrote it. If you're on a budget but aren't able to shoot your own video, solicit volunteer film students from a local college. Students are usually willing to work on such projects, which provide experience and something to show on their resumes.

## MySpace best practices

And here are several more rules of thumb for using MySpace as a publicity tool:

- **Try to keep your MySpace pages streamlined and clutter-free.** Make sure that anyone who sees it can easily discover your book and, if interested, buy it quickly. Put "buy this book" links so they'll appear on each page.

- **Keep your name in front of people by posting frequently to your MySpace blog and by sending a bulletin of the blog entry to all your friends.** But don't abuse the privilege – if you post too frequently without something of value, your friends will quickly decide to ignore you, or delete you from their list of friends.

- **Ignore folks on MySpace who try to sell *you* something you're uninterested in, or those who try to hook up for a date.**

Unless you're interested in this, it's best to focus on the friends who find value in your ideas and books. When you set up your MySpace page, it's easy to make clear you're not there for dating – that way you'll eliminate a lot of spam from unwanted "friends."

- **Don't feel obligated to accept every friend who zaps an invitation your way.** It's best to concentrate on having 50 friends you truly connect with, rather than having thousands of friends you quickly forget about.

- **To leverage MySpace as a professional asset, your page must look professional.** Your potential friends will check out your existing friends, so your MySpace utility will be undermined by having too many friends who have no connection to your niche. It's fine to have some oddballs in there, but be certain you have a clear connection with your Top 8 friends.

- **To keep the hits coming, you've got to maintain your MySpace page.** Throwing together a page and never visiting or tweaking it will do little good.

- **Don't promote your MySpace profile at the expense of your own domain.** MySpace is a great networking tool, but you don't want to depend on it exclusively. Perhaps someday MySpace will go out of business, begin charging high fees, or simply won't fit your image anymore. In any case, you can purchase an important insurance policy for only $9 a year by registering your own domain name and forwarding the traffic to your MySpace page—your domain registrar can handle this for you. Instead of printing your MySpace URL in your books and on business cards, you'll print your own domain, and you can forward the traffic to MySpace if you wish. Later, if you decide to focus your efforts elsewhere, you can take your traffic with you by forwarding it someplace else.

## Other places on MySpace

Book clubs are increasingly popular on MySpace, such as Teen Lit, **http://groups.myspace.com/teenlit**, founded by Sarah Mlynowski, author of *Frogs & French Kisses*. About 100 teenlit authors belong to the group.

At Memoirists Collective, authors hold contests offering readers the chance to get their own memoirs sold to a major trade publisher. See **www.myspace.com/thememoiristscollective**. The group has more than 1,000 members, or "friends." It was founded in 2006 by author Josh Kilmer-Purcell and four other newly published memoirists who met by networking on MySpace. Periodically the group holds contests, with winning memoir manuscripts passed on to the authors' editors at trade publishers.

The group serves as a sounding board for members and a place for authors and readers to meet and chat about their craft.

Here are examples of other authors who have applied their creativity to MySpace to generate their own book publicity:

**www.MySpace.com/TheSistaHood**

**Elisha Miranda** uses MySpace for grass-roots marketing of her debut teenlit novel *The Sista Hood*. She has a MySpace page for each character in the story, allowing readers to follow the lives of characters beyond the book's ending. She also sells a CD with music based on the novel.

**www.MySpace.com/CraftyChica**

**Kathy Cano Murillo**, author of five craft books, calls herself the "Crafty Chica." She specializes in Chicano and Mexican pop art, and is also a syndicated craft columnist for Gannett News Service. On her MySpace page, she advertises her books and promotes a three-day Carnival Cruise where readers can meet her and take classes on making the hip Latino-themed art featured in her latest title, *Crafty Chica's Art de la Soul*. Murillo is also finishing up her first novel.

## More social-networking sites

MySpace is just one of a growing number of social-networking sites. Amazon is an investor in **www.43Things.com**, which was founded by some ex-Amazon employees. On 43Things, members list goals, things they want to accomplish, and assign tags to help put them in touch with like-minded members.

Google owns another of these sites, **www.Orkut.com**. Others are **www.Friendster.com**, **www.LinkedIn.com**, and **www.Tribe.net**.

This sector of the Internet is growing and changing at a terrific rate, and bears watching. It's entirely possible that MySpace won't continue its overwhelming domination of Internet social networking indefinitely. A more likely scenario is that niche networks will emerge, splintering audiences into smaller sites focused on narrower interests. Someday, an entrepreneur will launch the "MySpace" of science fiction, romance, chicklit, or something else. Be on the lookout for up-and-coming networks in your sphere of interest. Or perhaps you'll have an idea for launching a network yourself.

# Tag – You're it!

*Tagging* is a relatively new but increasingly popular way for Internet users to organize things by using personal keywords. Tags can be used to label all kinds of items, including books, Web pages and pictures. Already, some are calling tags "the Internet's Dewey Decimal System."

For a book like *Gone With the Wind*, you might assign tags like "Civil War," "fiction," "epic," and "romance." It all depends on what the book means to you.

Users create tags for their own purposes, but they can be used by anyone. With enough people participating, tags can become an effortless, super-accurate recommendations system among like-minded people.

The site that popularized tagging was **www.Flickr.com**, a social site where users store, organize and share their digital photos. Instead of using a single category for organizing pictures—like a folder labeled "2005 Vacation"—members use one- or two-word tags like waterfall, solar eclipse, Houston, Joe or 2005. This way, photos can be grouped and discovered in multiple ways.

Tags are a form of *metadata*, which means, literally, "data about data." Tagging creates a *folksonomy*, a bottom-up method of categorization. *Taxonomies* are governed by experts like librarians and botanists who want to show hierarchical relationships. Folksonomies are built by amateurs but can be more helpful for users.

Folksonomies are gaining steam, aided by the easy exchange of ideas online. Often taxonomies aren't specific, flexible or current enough. Increasingly, people use tags to tap collective wisdom.

## Personal book tagging

A growing number of book lovers are using tags to provide their own way of classifying books. Amazon and some library catalogs have introduced user-generated tags to supplement hierarchical systems, like Library of Congress subject headings.

Book tagging enables anyone to assign trendy, granular labels to books with more authority than a librarian. For example, there's no library category or Amazon tab for *steampunk*, a subgenre of speculative fiction. But using tags, aficionados can dissect steampunk into all its sub-subgenres, including timepunk, bronzepunk, stonepunk and clockpunk—all very different animals to steampunkers.

Likewise, at least a half-dozen subgenres are within what many people call "queer fiction." But you won't find subject headings for any of it in a library. Instead, these books are shelved in "City Life" or "San Francisco," which doesn't help anyone find them. Traditional subject headings don't connect with personal identity, but tags can.

## Amazon tags

Why should authors care about tags? Because tags are an important new way for readers to discover your books. Tagging is an individual activity with global utility. Each of the 3.5 million books in Amazon's catalog could be assigned its own unique "category" yet reside in thousands of other categories at the same time.

Amazon added its tagging feature in 2005, and made it more prominent—higher on book detail pages—than its traditional category lists. Amazon tags are publicly viewable unless users designate them as private. You can manage your tags through a **Your Tags** field at the bottom of every Amazon page.

Authors and publishers can increase the visibility of their books by adding the obvious keywords appropriate to their book. Amazon tags are indexed by Google and other search engines.

As more book readers begin tagging, finding niche content will become easier than ever. Tags assigned to obscure books will be rare but instantly apparent. A few common tags will be used by huge numbers of users and visible to everyone: The five most-used tags on Amazon are DVD, music, books, fantasy and anime. Most tags, including the more useful ones, will be seldom used, such as *bizarre apocalpytacism,* Amazon's least-used tag. Many tags will be used by just a few people, perhaps assigned to only one book, enabling a niche of one.

As a reader, here are some ways you could use tags on Amazon:

- **Organize your books.** Tag the books you already own and organize them as you wish. If you don't agree with the category groups as Amazon has arranged them, make up your own. Tag the items that matter to you with categories you care about.

- **Remember books you're considering buying.** If one of your tagged books is intended for a Christmas gift, you can tag the book "Xmas" or "present"—tags that aren't very useful to others. Tags like "real best picture of 2004" are better.

- **Personalized book recommendations based on tags.** Go to "Your Store" and click on tags shown under the heading "Recommendations Based on Your Tags."

You can view all your tags on Amazon here:

**www.Amazon.com/gp/tagging/manage-tags**

Here you can add or delete tags, and designate them public or private. You can also edit or remove tags you've created by clicking on Edit from the book's product page.

You can view the tags for any Amazon customer who's made at least one purchase, unless they've chosen to keep their tags private.

## Amazon Media Library

You can also tag books within a personalized section of Amazon called Your Media Library:

**www.Amazon.com/gp/library**

Here you can view all your previous purchases and buy online access to eligible physical books you've purchased from Amazon. You can organize your Media Library by tagging individual books:

- Click on the book to select it. Bibliographic information will be displayed at the top of the screen.

- Any currently used tags for the book will be displayed just below.

- Click the Add button to enter tags. If you've created other tags previously, a list of similar tags is shown below the edit box.
- Type in a new tag or click a suggested tag and click OK to save.

Once you're using tags, try to be consistent, using the same tag to designate the same association. For example, don't use both "art deco" and "artdec" to tag the same kinds of things. For help, consult the list of your most frequently used tags, which pops up when you're tagging.

Although it's relatively new, Media Library could become the hub of Amazon's social-networking strategy, an avenue for readers to connect with others who have common interests.

## LibraryThing

**www.LibraryThing.com** was launched in 2005 and instantly became the No. 1 social-networking site devoted to bibliophiles. Like other popular social networks, LibraryThing has grown purely on word of mouth, not advertising.

Like other social sites, part of the fun at LibraryThing is belonging to a big club that lets you display how eclectic and singular your taste is. Meanwhile there's the chance you'll meet a few one-in-a-million literary soulmates who are passionate about the same books as you.

Spending time on LibraryThing is addictive because of all the interesting connections that surface, especially with obscure books. Entering your copy of Harry Potter won't move the needle. But when you enter your copy of *Environmental Kuznet Curves*, things get interesting.

Members enter their book collection simply by punching in the ISBNs. Then members can compare their whole collection—or individual rarities—against the collections of others. Ever wonder who else in the world has read that oddball book you love? On LibraryThing you'll know.

LibraryThing also has a book recommendation system that founder Tim Spalding claims is more accurate than Amazon's, simply because its users pay more attention. On LibraryThing, members input the books they want to drive their recommendations, no matter when or where they acquired them. Books you've purchased as gifts easily corrupt Amazon recommendations, and most users don't input the books they've purchased elsewhere.

Further, Amazon recommends only current books available through wholesalers, the ones it can sell. Since LibraryThing isn't a bookseller, it's free to recommend out-of-print books. Finally, LibraryThing recommendations are filtered, drawn from the collections of other users like you, not the whole universe. Harry Potter isn't recommended to everyone.

Another difference is LibraryThing's anonymity. Unlike a bookselling site, which must identify users to collect payments, LibraryThing knows only a user's log-on name—unless that member posts more information and makes it public. This gives members the freedom to list books and provide other information they'd rather not be associated with publicly.

As an author, you can build a special page on LibraryThing to show members what's on your bookshelf. To become a LibraryThing author, you must have at least one book listed at Amazon or the Library of Congress, and you or another member must add the book to LibraryThing. Also, you must catalog at least 50 books on LibraryThing, and you'll need a public account that allows comments on your profile. Get more details by sending e-mail to **Abby@LibraryThing.com**.

Whether LibraryThing will generate the same kind of demand for niche books as commercial networks like Amazon is unclear. But the potential for such user-generated recommendations is huge. The bookselling network **www.AbeBooks.com**, which sells new and out-of-print books, bought 40 percent of LibraryThing in 2006. AbeBooks will use LibraryThing's data to provide book recommendations to customers.

## Tag-based marketing

As an author or publisher, you should use tags to stay current on how people are finding and sharing information in your field. For example, you can subscribe to RSS feeds to monitor how consumers tag information related to your books and topic areas. For example, to keep tabs on organic fruit, you could bookmark this page:

**http://del.icio.us/tag/organic+fruit**

By bookmarking this page, you'll get updates on interesting links consumers are discovering and sharing about "organic fruit." You'll have a global focus group working for you 24 hours a day, seven days a week.

Or let's imagine you want to monitor all the books to which Amazon users assign the tag "murder mystery." You can watch:

**www.Amazon.com/gp/tagging/glance/murder+mystery**

Should you tag your own books? Certainly, but anyone using tags for marketing should be transparent about it, says Steve Rubel, author of the blog Micro Persuasion. In other words, if you're plugging your own book, don't pretend you're an uninterested bystander. Don't hide your identity, and don't spam.

## Problems with tags

One weakness of tags is that the same tag can mean two completely different things to different people. For example, a recent memoir by CNN correspondent Anderson Cooper is tagged by various Amazon users with "news memoir," "blue eyes," and "hunk." Since "hunk" is a tag with many possible meanings, it appears on many products with seemingly no connection—like a movie starring Russell Crowe, the DVD *Forrest Gump*, heavy sweaters, and books about the "chunky" clothing style.

Conversely, various people will assign different tags to the same thing—one person may tag photos of their dog "cocker spaniel" while another user tags the same photo "canines." A search for the tag "dogs" might not turn up either photo. With books, an Amazon user may assign the tag "Christmas" to a book about baseball, meaning that she intends to buy it as a Christmas gift. Meanwhile, customers using the tag "Christmas" to search for Christmas books will be frustrated.

Like any valuable tool, tags can be abused too. If tagging goes mainstream, spammers will try exploiting tags by adding their irrelevant tags to popular items.

Tags aren't necessarily linked with semantics. So the word "blow" could be used as a tag for wind, cocaine, sucking, breath, or a picture of a tornado, or the sound of air rushing. The user of the tag, not a search engine, decides how the meaning fits for them.

Advocates of tagging assert these fears are overblown. With enough users, tags become self-correcting, so inappropriate or useless tags will be drowned out by the good ones.

Whether it's Amazon, LibraryThing, or perhaps Google, whoever builds the biggest collection of tags will have an amazing insight into how people think about information, and will have a important tool for bookselling—the most detailed, current, and useful book index in history.

# Advanced Amazon tools

While advertising is rarely a cost-effective marketing technique for books, online *paid placement* can be a useful tactic if it delivers your message to your target audience and delivers results. Since Amazon has such a large share of book buyers, it offers some of the best opportunities for showcasing your book.

## Buy X, Get Y

You can increase the odds of buyers finding your book by paying at least $750 a month to display it with a complementary book in Amazon's Buy X Get Y program, known as BXGY. The primary benefit is your book's cover is prominently displayed on the detail page of a related book under the heading **Best Value**. Customers who buy both books get an additional 5 percent discount.

You'll pay more for a pairing with popular books. Amazon charges $1,000 a month for pairing with a book with a sales rank of 1 to 250, and $750 a month for pairing with slower-selling books.

An ideal BXGY campaign would pair your title with Amazon's No. 1 bestseller, so long as that bestseller appealed precisely to your audience. The stronger the Amazon Sales Rank of the paired title, the more people will see your promotion, and the more traffic will be redirected to your book's detail page. But if the paired title isn't relevant to your book, it won't work. Pairing your book with the latest installment of *Harry Potter* would bring a ton of exposure, but it wouldn't produce many sales, unless your book was aimed at the same readers.

You can find BXGY candidates by browsing Amazon's category bestseller lists and searching Amazon's book section for relevant keywords. Use the "Sort by" drop-down menu on the right to sift the books according to sales rank, publication date, and price. After browsing the search results, use Amazon's Search Inside the Book feature to get more information about the content of the titles. You can also browse for potential pairings at this Top Sellers link:

**www.Amazon.com/exec/obidos/tg/new-for-you/top-sellers/-/books**

Some publishers have tried pairing two of their own titles for BXGY, figuring it would boost sales of both books, but it doesn't. The main value of BXGY is sending readers to your book's detail page who might not find it otherwise. You can pair your title with only one other title at a time.

Publishers can participate in BXGY under Amazon's "small vendor" program if they have less than $1 million in annual sales on Amazon by applying at:

**www.Amazon.com/exec/obidos/subst/misc/co-op/small-vendor-faq.html**

## Weaknesses of BXGY

Amazon doesn't provide any figures on the success rates of BXGY promotions. Anecdotally, many publishers complain that while the program increases sales a bit, the revenue from those increased sales rarely covers the fees. However, BXGY is a tool some publishers use to spark initial word of mouth for a book, and in that sense it can be considered an investment. As discussed previously, increasing your sales on Amazon often leads to more success, bringing years of steady sales.

Often BXGY offers aren't compelling for buyers. Customers don't qualify for the program's 5 percent discount unless they purchase both the books new from Amazon; purchases of used copies don't count. For this reason, pairing your title with an older classic isn't effective if there's a plentiful supply of used or discounted copies. Buyers don't have much incentive to buy both books at full retail when they can get one deeply discounted.

Amazon offers more paid placement programs to large publishers, who can buy spots on Amazon's home page, category pages, and in specialized stores and seasonal lists such as "Back to School" or "Top Cookbooks of 2007." However, these placements aren't available under Amazon's Small Vendor program.

## Free paired placement

You can get BXGY-like exposure without paying fees if your book sales are strong, relative to other titles in your category. Amazon pairs your book with a related title in a display nearly identical to BXGY's **Best Value** , but in this case it's called **Better Together**.

To see this in action, go to any book's detail page on Amazon. Under the heading **Better Together**, you'll see the book paired with another book, much like BXGY, albeit without the extra 5 percent discount.

If your book is the best-selling title in its niche, your book can appear on the Better-Together spot for several other related titles—another example of how strong sales on Amazon create more exposure for you.

## Single New Product e-mails

Another Amazon placement opportunity is Single New Product e-mails, or SNPs. Amazon sends e-mails announcing your newly published title to customers who've purchased similar books or titles by certain authors.

Using a list of ISBNs suggested by the publisher, Amazon creates a pool of recipients who receive an e-mail highlighting your book, with links to buy it from the site. Amazon targets 5,000 to 10,000 recipients per mailing.

SNPs provide a unique marketing opportunity to publishers who don't have a large e-mail list of prospective book buyers they can advertise to. By contrast, most companies that offer e-mail lists for rental are used by spammers, and using their lists might result in more complaints than book sales.

The cost for small vendors with less than $1 million in annual sales on Amazon is $1,500 per title per SNP mailing. Titles are eligible for SNPs only during the 90 days following their publication date. To schedule SNPs, publishers must complete an SNP nomination form a few months before the publication date and commit to a certain month for the promotion.

## Amazon Connect

In 2006 Amazon launched its Connect feature, enabling authors to send blog posts directly to readers on Amazon's site. Your posts appear in several places—on your book's detail page, your Amazon profile—and buyers of your book receive an alert on Amazon's home page in a box called a *plog*.

Your Amazon Connect blog is a unique opportunity to communicate with new readers, and requires a different approach than you'd use with longtime readers on your own Web site. Visitors at your Amazon blog will include mostly first-time readers, who might feel as if they're butting into the middle of a conversation.

Your Amazon blog provides a great opportunity to introduce yourself to readers, says literary agent Matt Wagner, founder of Fresh Books:

> Amazon Connect is your chance to stand next to your reader at the bookstore. The key is to be polite and not screw it up!
>
> The key to writing an Amazon blog is not overdoing it. Understand that your readers are here to buy a book, not read a blog. This is not the place for long, drawn-out entries about your personal life or about the process of writing your next book. This is the place to put your book in context for readers who might be looking at your competition. A great place to start is: "Why I wrote this book."

Amazon Connect blogs also provide a way for you to stay in touch with readers who haven't yet committed to buying your book—or people who might be interested in your next book. Readers can subscribe to your Amazon blog in three ways:

- Browsing the directory, **Amazon.com/gp/arms/directory**.
- Clicking the yellow button labeled **Add to your Plog** from the Amazon Connect portion of your book's detail page.
- Visiting your author Profile page and clicking Add posts to my plog in the blue box on the top right of the page.

You can also use your Amazon blog to refer visitors to your own Web site. Some authors do this by posting only the first paragraph of their post at Amazon, and asking readers to click through to their own site to continue reading.

You can get more information and apply for an Amazon blog here:

**www.Amazon.com/Connect**

After you apply for Amazon Connect, there's a verification procedure where your publisher or agent certifies you're actually the book author and are authorized to post materials about it on Amazon.

One fast way to add content to your Amazon Connect blog is by repurposing material you've already used at your own blog. However, if you use exactly the same material without much rewriting, Google and other search engines may flag the post as "duplicate content." More on that later.

## Listmania

Listmania lists allow any Amazon user—readers, authors, music-lovers, movie buffs—to create lists of their favorite items organized by theme. Listmanias appear in various places on Amazon, like product detail pages and alongside search results. Listmanias that mention your book can expose your title to thousands of potential readers on Amazon, and can even appear in Google search results.

Listmanias are ranked by popularity among shoppers, based on viewership and the number of votes calling it "helpful." For example, one popular list is dedicated to novelist Nick Hornby, and was compiled by one of his fans. Under each novel is a pithy quote from the Listmania author, just enough to convey the gist of each book and why it appears. The list includes most of Hornby's books, other books Hornby edited or wrote introductions for, and a few other novels by writers with similar styles. See this list at:

**www.Amazon.com/gp/richpub/listmania/fullview/1X1GGDBXARHZ6**

See the 100 most popular Listmanias here:

**www.Amazon.com/gp/richpub/listmania/toplists**

As an author, you're free to recommend books yourself with a Listmania list, mentioning up to 25 books in your list.

Niche books stand to gain the most from Listmanias. The more focused a Listmania is, the more helpful it is to buyers hungry for specific information—so the more likely it is to be noticed, read carefully, and acted on. Niche Listmanias have less competition—Amazon can show only so many "Harry Potter" Listmanias while the thousands of similar lists wait in a queue. But your Listmania about "Organic Strawberries" may pop up in front of every single customer looking for a relevant book.

To write a Listmania, click on the link at the bottom of your Amazon profile page, "More to Explore." Or start your list by clicking on the link Create Your Own List on an existing Listmania. Then:

1. Go to your Amazon Profile at: **www.Amazon.com/gp/pdp**.
2. Near the bottom of the middle column, in the section **More to Explore**, click Listmania Lists.
3. Click Create your first one now or Create another list.
4. Enter a title for your list and enter your "qualifications" such as "Avid reader" or "Book author." For your title, think of a blurb that will catch the eye of anyone shopping for a related book.
5. Enter ISBNs for the books for your list and a short comment for each.
6. Click the **Preview** button and check for typos.
7. Edit your list, and when satisfied, click the button **Publish list**. You can edit it later if you wish.

Your Listmania lists will appear on your Profile and in search results related to items on your list. From your Profile, you'll have the option of editing your lists or deleting them.

## Publicize your book

On your book's product page at Amazon is a link Tell a Friend. A form will appear on your browser with the boilerplate message:

Hello,

I found this item at Amazon.com and thought you might find it of interest.

Ask recipients to forward the message to their friends. But don't go overboard: This form isn't to be used for bulk "promotional" purposes, according to Amazon. So don't use the Tell a Friend feature for people you don't know or anyone who might complain about the message. You don't want to be accused of sending spam.

## So You'd Like to . . . guides

Have you ever wished you could submit a how-to essay to your local newspaper that demonstrates your expertise and helps publicize your book? You can accomplish much the same feat on Amazon by writing a *So You'd Like to ...* guide, which could be read by more people than a newspaper article.

Amazon's *So You'd Like to ...* guides somewhat resemble Listmania, but are more like tutorials. They're time-consuming and require considerably more original writing than Listmanias, but are consulted often, especially in niche topics. A short excerpt from your book might serve as the basis of a guide.

For example, you could write a guide called "Beginner's Guide to Growing Organic Fruit." In the course of writing your guide, you can link to items from Amazon's garden section, general gardening reference books, and your title *Organic Strawberries*.

To include non-book merchandise in your guide you'll need to look up the 10-digit ASIN (Amazon Standard Identification Number) that appears on the item's detail page under the heading **Product Details**.

To get started writing a guide, go to your Amazon profile at **www.Amazon.com/gp/pdp**. Near the bottom of the middle column, in the section labeled **More to Explore**, click on So You'd Like To ... Guides, then click on Create a guide. As you compose your guide, insert book ISBNs wherever you want to refer to a book in this format:

**<ASIN: 1234567890>**

You should use the characters "ASIN" even if you're using a book ISBN. Don't enter the book title, because Amazon will insert it automatically.

Guides must include at least three ISBNs or ASINs and may have a maximum of 50. The first three ISBNs/ASINs you mention in your guide will become featured items that appear at the top of your guide when it appears on Amazon's site.

Break up your guide into sections every few paragraphs by inserting a subheading like this:

**<HEADLINE: (Type your headline here)>**

Before finishing, copy your text into a word processor and spell-check it. After you're finished writing and editing your guide, click on the **Publish** button.

Later you can add books or more content to your guides by editing them. From your Profile at **www.Amazon.com/gp/pdp**, click So You'd Like To ... Guides near the bottom of the middle column, then click the **Edit** button on the right of the guide you wish to change.

## Search Inside the Book

If you walked into a bookstore, and all the books were shrink-wrapped shut, would you be inclined to spend much time shopping? Probably not. Yet Amazon operated with this handicap for its first eight years—customers couldn't actually see inside the books.

In 2003 Amazon enrolled the first 120,000 books in Search Inside, enabling buyers to view sample pages and search the complete text, providing millions more ways for buyers to stumble onto your book.

Previously, buyers could search only for words in book titles. With Search Inside, anyone searching for words contained somewhere in your book can find it, even without knowing the title or author name. For example, if a shopper searches Amazon for *Eleanor Rigby*, the top three results are books whose titles contain Eleanor Rigby. Then come another 568 books that mention Eleanor Rigby on at least one page.

Like nearly every Amazon innovation, Search Inside was resisted by many publishers, who insisted it would hurt book sales. Why, they argued, would anyone buy a book—especially cookbooks, travel guides, or other references—if they could get the pages they wanted free? But after Amazon reported average sales boosts of 9 percent for titles enrolled in Search Inside, most publishers signed up.

Amazon uses Search Inside to sell books just like Baskin-Robbins sells ice cream: by giving people a sample right when they're in a position to buy, says Amazon chief executive Jeff Bezos:

> “ If you went to the middle of Central Park on a hot day and let people sample your ice cream, they *might* come back later [to your store] and buy some. But if you let them sample ice cream right next to the cash register—inside the Baskin-Robbins—you're definitely going to increase sales. So the idea is to literally let people look inside the book and find what they're looking for.

Bezos concedes Search Inside doesn't convert everyone into a buyer. Many people use it as a research tool without paying, but were probably not likely buyers anyway.

Amazon builds safeguards into Search Inside to prevent customers from reading large portions of a book without buying it. Users must register with a credit card first, and can view no more than 20 percent of any particular book. The text displayed on the screen is a low-resolution image, and it can't be copied into a word processor.

Search Inside also provides a unique marketing opportunity for crafty writers able to hook readers with their first sentence. Amazon displays your initial sentence hyperlinked, so interested readers can click straight through to your whole introduction. If your book has a long first sentence, only its first 125 characters are displayed on the detail page, followed by an ellipsis.

To enroll in Search Inside, go to:

**www.Amazon.com/publishers**

Then click the link for Search Inside. The publisher must initiate participation; a distributor can't enroll your book.

## Statistically Improbable Phrases

Statistically Improbable Phrases is an Amazon feature launched in 2005 to identify a book's most unique word combinations compared to other books indexed by Search Inside's program. SIPs are one more potential way for readers to find relevant books, especially niche content.

For books enrolled in Search Inside, you'll find SIPs displayed on the book's detail page under the heading **Inside This Book**. For example, the book *The Da Vinci Code* has these SIPs:

- cilice belt
- seeded womb
- pope interred
- lame saint
- lettered dials
- tracking dot
- inlaid rose
- corporal mortification
- rosewood box
- sacred feminine
- depository bank
- royal bloodline
- stone cylinder
- sweater pocket

Amazon's SIPs are hyperlinked, so clicking on them brings up a display of other books containing the same SIPs. From here, users can click through to see where the SIP appears in each book, using the Amazon Online Reader.

It's surprising to see how seldom certain word combinations occur among millions of books. For example, the first SIP given for *The Da*

*Vinci Code,* "cilice belt," appears in only one other book—a book about *The Da Vinci Code.*

Amazon is considering ways to merge SIPs with its recommendation system, or use SIPs for new kinds of services, like answering questions using authoritative texts.

Along with SIPs, Amazon displays other text statistics, including a list of capitalized phrases and a list of the 100 most frequently appearing words in the book, called the *concordance.*

How helpful these extra features are for shoppers isn't yet clear. "When we expose new features, we measure how they change the customer's behavior," says Amazon's Bezos. "For example, does it take the customer fewer steps to find what he or she needs? This is hard, because you are measuring human behavior. There are some things that customers are delighted about immediately, and there are other things that they have to get used to."

## Writing book reviews

For nonfiction writers, half your battle is establishing a reputation as a thought leader in your field. One way to build your reputation is by writing reviews of other books in your field. Writing a compelling review of a popular book can enhance your reputation and expose your name to many more readers.

Don't hype your own book or mention its title in your review of other books. This is viewed by many as blatant self-promotion, and can result in your review being deleted by Amazon.

However, many authors add their book titles to their Amazon pen names displayed with reviews, such as John Steinbeck, author of 'The Grapes of Wrath.' To change the way your name is displayed, go to your Amazon Profile at **www.Amazon.com/gp/pdp**. In the left column, in the **About Me** section, click change name.

To write a review, from the book's detail page on Amazon, scroll down to the section labeled **Spotlight Reviews**, then click the link Write an online review.

The maximum length of reviews is 1,000 words, and the recommended length is 75 to 300 words. The title of your review is limited to 60 characters. A good review focuses on the book's content, including whether you liked or disliked a book, and why.

Amazon strongly discourages the following elements in customer reviews:

- Spoiling a story's ending or revealing crucial plot elements.
- Dates of promotional tours or lectures that become outdated.
- Commenting on previous reviews of the book (other reviews might be edited or deleted in the future).
- Profanity or cruel remarks.
- Single-word reviews.
- Contact information such as phone numbers, addresses or URLs.
- Discussing the book's price, availability, or shipping information.
- Asking people to "vote" for your review.

Check your review for spelling and typos by running the text through a word processor. Break up your text with a blank line between each paragraph to add white space.

Often reviews show up immediately on the book's detail page, but sometimes it takes several days. To ask about the status of a review, write to **community-help@amazon.com**.

The more helpful your review is to Amazon users, the more often it will be voted "helpful" and have an impact. Spotlight Reviews have the most impact since they appear first. Your review has a better chance of becoming a Spotlight if it's submitted soon after the book's publication date, and after a few other reviews have already appeared.

Be honest in your reviews. As a practical matter, though, it's best to avoid skewering competing authors. Enormous feuds result from negative reviews posted on Amazon by competitors, and your time and energy can be better spent improving your own work.

## ProductWikis

Amazon launched ProductWikis in April 2006, allowing customers to write their own articles, or wikis, on any product page. The Amazon wikis resemble user-generated content popularized by Wikipedia.org, a free online encyclopedia.

The concept behind wikis is that anyone can write one, and that anyone else can come along later and correct mistakes. It's unclear how useful wikis will be for Amazon shoppers—will shoppers want to read miscellaneous writings by other shoppers, or care enough to correct mistakes?

Wikis are supposed to differ from book reviews and other user-generated content in one important way: Writers are supposed to stick to facts, and avoid injecting their opinions.

What could hurt the utility of wikis is their misuse by spammers. And there's nothing to prevent competing authors or publishers from adding false information. Wikis are supposed to be self-correcting, but experience shows this doesn't always happen.

## Customer Discussions

Customer Discussions are a relatively new feature on Amazon allowing customers to ask questions, share insights, and give opinions about books and other products. However, since this feature appears near the bottom of increasingly crowded Amazon detail pages, customer discussions are used very infrequently. No mechanism exists to notify authors or publishers of questions requiring a follow-up.

## BookSurge

BookSurge is an Amazon subsidiary that provides print-on-demand (POD) service. POD is used by a variety of publishers who prefer to print certain titles in small batches, rather than ordering a large quantity of traditionally printed books, requiring immediate capital, shipping, and storage.

BookSurge is marketed as a service for self-publishing authors, but is just one of several options. For a full discussion of the merits of POD versus offset printing—and self-publishing versus trade publishing—read *Print-on-Demand Book Publishing* by Morris Rosenthal.

## Your Amazon profile

Few know it, but each Amazon customer has a Profile page. If you have an Amazon account, you can see your profile at:

**www.Amazon.com/gp/pdp**

Your Amazon profile is a convenient place to access and manage content you've posted to Amazon, like book reviews, Listmanias, blog posts, and *So You'd Like To...* guides.

For book authors, an Amazon profile provides yet more opportunities to educate shoppers about your titles, and to refer them to your own Web site if you wish. You can upload your photograph, post a short biography, and add several personal details.

If you have an Amazon Connect blog, your posts are displayed on your Amazon profile, along with some anonymous feedback from readers, such as "5 of 6 readers who voted liked this post."

On the right column of your profile, you can set preferences for display of your Amazon Wishlists and previous purchases. By default, your previous Amazon purchases are publicly viewable, but you can make them private.

## Amazon friends

Like profiles, "Amazon friends" is a little-known feature, but is gaining prominence as the company emphasizes community features. Designating someone your Amazon friend provides an easy way for you to track his or her community participation on Amazon. Depending on the privacy settings on both profiles, you can view each other's recent purchases, Wish Lists, upcoming birthdays, and e-mail address.

Adding someone as an Amazon friend can help you find people interested in networking or receiving a review copy of your book. To make an Amazon friend invitation, scroll about two-thirds of the way down your profile page, **www.Amazon.com/gp/pdp**.

You'll see a heading for **Amazon Friends & Interesting People** and a search box where you can input names or e-mail addresses. Clicking on the person's name or e-mail address allows you to send a message that will be forwarded by Amazon.

Amazon users have three options in responding to a friend invitation:

- **Accept** – Both members become each other's Amazon friend and appear on each other's list of Friends.

- **Decline** – The sender's invitation is removed from a list of pending invitations on the invitee's profile. The sender isn't notified the invitation is declined, and is free to send future invitations.
- **Decline and block** – Declines the invitation and prevents future Friends invitations. The sender's name appears in a "Blocked People" list visible to you on your profile, and you have the option of unblocking them later.
- **Ignore** – The default option, and probably the most popular. The recipient ignores the Friends invitation and deletes the e-mail.

Amazon users have the option of receiving friend invitations only from people who know their e-mail address and enter it correctly into the invitation form. Here's how to manage this setting:

1. On your profile page, scroll down the middle column to the section labeled **Amazon Friends & Interesting People**.
2. Click See your pending invitations.
3. At the bottom, in the section labeled **Blocking Preference**, check the box **Block invitations from people who don't know my e-mail address** and click the yellow button **Save preferences**.

## Interesting people

Amazon's Interesting People feature lets you bookmark authors or reviewers you're interested in, and enables you to see their latest Amazon activity on your Profile page—new book reviews, tagging activity, etc. To add someone to your interesting people list, go to their profile page and, in the box labeled **Your Actions**, click the link Add to Interesting People. You can search for people to add to your list by selecting **People** from the search pull-down menu at the top left corner of your profile page.

## Fine-tuning book recommendations

Because so many sales can result from Amazon recommendations, it's worth spending a few minutes looking under the hood. Here's a shortcut to your Amazon recommendations:

**www.Amazon.com/yourstore**

On the left, click Books to filter out other types of products. Now, directly below each of the recommended books, you'll see the reason it's being recommended, such as: **Recommended because you purchased [TITLE].**

For each book recommended, you can refine the system by indicating:

- Whether you own the book.
- Whether you're just "not interested" in the recommended book.
- Your rating for the book on a scale of 1 to 5, with 5 meaning "I love it."

Few Amazon customers take the time to confirm this raw data in Amazon's recommendations engine, and as a result it can spit out some wacky suggestions. If you've purchased books for children or friends that you wouldn't read yourself, the result is faulty recommendations.

In some cases, Amazon will guess correctly which of your purchases are gifts—for example, when you ship a book to a different address—and excludes them from recommendations.

Here's how to exclude other inappropriate books from your recommendations:

- Near the top of your recommendations list is the text, "These recommendations are based on items you own and more."
- Clicking you own shows the list of books Amazon knows you've purchased.
- To exclude books from the recommendations system, uncheck the box labeled **Use to make recommendations**.

You can also improve your recommendations by letting Amazon know about books you've purchased elsewhere.

The star ratings you assign to books on this list won't be visible to other Amazon users, but the ratings can affect which books get recommended to whom and how often.

As you scroll through the list of books, be on the lookout for quality books you've read that are complementary to your book. When you find one, check the box **Use to make recommendations** and assign it a 5-star rating. This will encourage Amazon to recommend your book to other users with your same buying and rating history. This will help seed Amazon's recommendation system for your book.

Here's a way to further jump-start your book in Amazon's recommendation system: Buy other books published in your niche, along with your own book. Ask your friends and family to buy them also. This will inject your title into the recommendation engine. It won't dictate the long-term position of your book; that will depend on the independent actions of many thousands of customers. But those paired purchases, if relevant, can surface your title in Amazon recommendations weeks earlier than might otherwise occur.

## Pricing and discounting strategies

Much of your exposure on Amazon depends on how many sales you rack up. The more sales, the more often Amazon gives your book free exposure in its Also-Bought lists, Better-Together spots, and recommendations on its Web site and in e-mails. It's a virtuous cycle, one that can make a successful book even more successful.

For most of Amazon's history, this system has been neutral—your exposure was determined purely by sales. The playing field was level. It didn't matter whether a book was by a famous author or an unknown, or published in New York or in your neighbor's basement. It didn't matter whether the book was a pocket-sized paperback or a leather-bound collector's edition. Amazon's customers voted by buying, and books with the best sales got the most exposure.

In mid-2006, however, Amazon changed this system, perhaps with an eye toward improving its quarterly financial statements. Amazon boosted exposure of expensive books and those with big wholesale discounts. Meanwhile, it cut exposure for books with lower prices and so-called "short" discounts. In other words, Amazon began showing customers not necessarily the *best* recommendation—the book most popular among similar buyers—but recommendations filtered according to how profitable the books are for Amazon to sell.

It's unclear exactly what formula Amazon is using to filter its recommendations. Some publishers believe a book's list price is the more important factor, while others believe the wholesale discount matters more. Whatever the formula is, apparently it's a secret. In fact, at least one Amazon executive has flatly denied the company is filtering recommendations at all, although the effects of the practice have become clear to many publishers who track their Amazon sales closely. Many of those publishers are irritated that Amazon seems to be favoring publishers who give bigger wholesale discounts than the 40 percent they have traditionally given to brick-and-mortar bookstores.

It's also unclear whether Amazon's practice of recommendation filtering is a wise long-term strategy. Some customers may begin ignoring recommendations and buy fewer books if they realize that certain books are being recommended mainly because they're expensive. After all, buyers who pay close attention to Amazon's book recommendations tend to be the company's most profitable customers.

In any case, it seems that publishers who want to boost exposure of their titles on Amazon should consider raising their list price and offering generous wholesale discounts of perhaps 55 percent, instead of short discounts, such as 25 percent.

# Social search

In the mid 1990s, Yahoo, the first popular Web portal, guided most Internet traffic with a simple hand-picked menu of sites. Yahoo's editors decided which Web sites were worth pointing to, and that's where the traffic went. At the time, it seemed like a good system, and much more efficient than search engines, which tended to spit out mountains of irrelevant results. Back then, it sometimes seemed easier to find a needle in a haystack than to find anything with a search engine.

Then Google built a better mousetrap. Instead of relying on humans to figure out which content is best, Google's computers determined relevance and authority. Google's PageRank system considers not only the words contained on a Web page, but also how many related sites link in. Each incoming link is a vote on a page's importance, helping it rise to the top of Google's search results.

As good as Google's system is, however, it can't always deliver relevant results, particularly for specialized content. Sometimes providing good search results requires direct human brainpower, something provided by *social search* tools. Social search works best in deep niches, where people who truly understand the content render judgments. In these cases, social search can be more accurate than Google's algorithmic search, which counts links only.

Why should authors care about social search? Because more and more people are using it to find the exact content they want.

Here's what can happen if your book's Web site or blog is mentioned favorably on a social search service—a flood of 5,000 to 10,000 visitors can come to your site within hours. This crowd can include thousands of folks highly passionate about your topic, and those nearly impossible to reach through traditional advertising or publicity.

Dozens of popular sites have emerged in the past few years providing tools for search, social networking, and social bookmarking:

## del.icio.us

**http://del.icio.us** was launched in 2004 and is a dominant social bookmarking site. It's a handy way for people to store their favorite Web bookmarks online where they're portable, instead of on the PC, confined to one machine.

For example, a student writing a dissertation might use del.icio.us to track all their source materials and commentary. Instead of having a hard-to-read list of bookmarks in a drop-down menu on their Web browser, users just consult their del.icio.us page to view their favorite Web resources, along with their own annotations.

To organize their bookmarks, del.icio.us users tag them with personalized keywords, like a folksonomy, instead of using a hierarchical taxonomy or set categories. This makes it easier for del.icio.us users to find relevant resources intuitively.

But here's the ultimate value of social bookmarking: the ability to share bookmarks with others, instantly tapping into collective wisdom. For example, let's imagine you want to learn about tropical fish. From the del.icio.us home page, you search for "tropical fish." Instead of finding only the most *universally popular* sites Google shows you, on del.icio.us you find the *favorite* resources of tropical-fish fanatics. These are the resources valued by the people with experience, the people who eat, breathe and sleep tropical fish.

Shared resources are the ones with real word of mouth, not just a certain number of links or brute-force advertising. The results are the best in the judgment of those who know the most. There's no substitute for recommendations by people who've consumed the content and found it important, useful or entertaining.

*Search* is what you do when you know what you're looking for. *Discovery* is how you find what you didn't know existed.

## Smart crowds

When del.icio.us users save a Web page as a bookmark, they're "voting" for the page, much as Google's PageRank measures how popular a page is by counting incoming links. But with social bookmarks, individuals vote. With social sites, everyone votes, not just Webmasters and bloggers. Since individual Internet users vastly outnumber Webmasters or bloggers, the collective wisdom is much richer.

Once someone mentions you on del.icio.us—by bookmarking your book, your blog, or your Web site—it's much easier for people to find you, and you'll get a new stream of people coming to your site who are already interested in what you have to say.

You can hope that people will take it on themselves to bookmark you on del.icio.us, or you can make it easy for them. You can configure your blog to automatically insert a small **add to del.icio.us** button to the bottom of all your posts. Every reader who clicks the button casts another vote for you. For instructions on adding these buttons, see:

**www.publisher.yahoo.com/social_media_tools**

Del.icio.us was purchased by Yahoo in 2005.

## Vertical search

Another example of a social search tool is a *Swicki*, which improves and personalizes its results based on feedback from your site's users.

For example, imagine you publish a blog about labor unions. Your visitors frequently perform keyword searches using the word "labor" to find what they're looking for. A universal search for "labor" would produce many unhelpful results—content about pregnancy, birthing, premature births, and maternity leave.

By installing a Swicki on your site, users can customize their search results. They can vote up the relevant results they see—those on labor unions—and vote down the irrelevant results. The search engine learns from its users.

*Swicki* is a play on the words search and wiki, implying that its value comes from user input. The tool is provided free by a company called Eurekster. It can also produce some additional income for your site, if you elect to show the paid ads Swickis offers. For more information, see:

**www.Swicki.com**

You'll be able to design the look of your Swicki and receive a snippet of code to insert the Swicki into your site—the entire process takes about 20 minutes.

Another popular vertical search tool is provided by Rollyo, which promises to help users "roll your own" search engine. For details, visit:

**www.Rollyo.com**

Google is getting into the personalized-search field too. In late 2006, it began testing Google Customized Search, which is linked to its AdSense program. You can specify the Web sites you want searched and integrate its search box and results into your own site. See:

**www.Google.com/coop/cse**

## Amazon Search Suggestions

"Search Suggestions" is a feature launched in 2006 enabling anyone with an Amazon account to add a bit of human intelligence to the site's search engine. On each book detail page, the link Make a Search Suggestion allows users to recommend tying a book to specific keywords. Users also explain why the keywords are relevant and will help people find the book.

One way for an author to take advantage of Search Suggestions is to link their book with relevant words and expressions that don't appear in its title or subtitle, or perhaps even the full text. For example, let's imagine you've written a book about predicting hurricanes. A year after your book goes on sale, the most damaging hurricane in history, a storm named Zelda, devastates the Florida coast. By entering the Search Suggestion "Hurricane Zelda," more buyers would find your book, even though it didn't contain "Zelda."

Once your Search Suggestion is approved, when customers search using your keywords, the book appears in search results along with your relevancy explanation.

For example, one Amazon customer submitted a search suggestion for Shakespeare's play *Macbeth*. Now Macbeth appears when customers search for "The Scottish Play." The relevancy explanation is shown next to a link to the book: "Theater superstition dictates that 'Macbeth' is referred to as 'the Scottish play.'"

Another example: Searching for "stolen data" now returns the book, *I.T. Wars: Managing the Business-Technology Weave in the New Millennium.*

Adding human intelligence to book searches could be a big help for finding material in niche topic areas. However, it seems a feature like this could be misused by spammers and practical jokers, so it will be interesting to see whether Amazon can police the system effectively. However, several types of Search Suggestions are prohibited:

- Profanity, obscenities, or spiteful remarks.
- Commenting on other search suggestions (other suggestions and their position in search results can change).
- Phone numbers, mail addresses, URLs.
- Availability, price, or alternative ordering/shipping information.
- Time-sensitive material such as interviews or concerts.
- Suggestions which may be "controversial, politically or otherwise."

## Digg

**www.Digg.com** is a news community run by amateur news buffs instead of professional news editors. Members submit items of note they've found somewhere on the Web and vote for the ones they like. A typical entry might read: "A Windmill for Your Backyard? A new, affordable wind turbine promises to help homeowners fight rising energy costs." Readers would click through to the site or blog, read the original article, then vote it up (digg it) or down (undigg).

If your book or Web site gets voted up on Digg, you can expect a crush of visitors within minutes.

Originally Digg was narrowly focused on technology news, but in 2006 it expanded into world news, entertainment, politics, and other topics. Members pride themselves on unearthing noteworthy items that might be overlooked by traditional news sources.

Items are assigned to a category such as technology, business, gaming or entertainment. If a story receives enough votes, it's promoted to the site's home page, where it's often read by hundreds of thousands of members who often click through to the blog or Web site for further information, or perhaps blog about it themselves.

## Netscape

America Online/Netscape launched a Digg-style, user-driven news site in 2006 at **www.netscape.com**.

## Flickr

**www.Flickr.com** is a social bookmarking site focusing solely on photographs. Amateur and professional photographers upload their favorite photos to share with friends and strangers, who can assign tags and add comments. Yahoo bought Flickr in 2005.

## YouTube

YouTube is similar to Flickr but primarily features amateur and professional video content. After uploading, users can add comments, tags and link to favorite videos from their own Web site. Google agreed to buy YouTube in 2006.

## Popurls

**www.Popurls.com** is like a "greatest hits" of about 15 of the most highly trafficked social bookmarking sites, updated frequently.

## Listible

**www.Listible.com** is a site featuring lists of users' favorite Web sites resources classified by tags such as "design," "movie," "opensource," or "firefox." Lists are popular with many Web users. Users can rate the items on the list and post comments.

# Google, Amazon, digital content

Already dominant in the search-engine business, Google is becoming an increasingly important ally to publishers and booksellers—or a threat, depending on your point of view. A growing share of Web users use Google to find what they're searching for online, so Google is a crucial source of new visitors to author and publisher sites.

Meanwhile Google is evolving into an online marketplace connecting book shoppers and publishers, and could become a major competitor to Amazon in book retailing, both with e-books and physical books.

## Google Book Search

Google's Book Search program allows publishers to make previews of their books available on the Web, much like Amazon's Search Inside the Book program. Users can search the full text of books that Google scans and stores after receiving submissions from participating publishers at:

**www.Books.Google.com**

For each participating book, Google provides links to online vendors who sell physical copies of the book. Google won't say how many books are enrolled in the program, other than to say it's in the "hundreds of thousands."

Google Book Search provides free worldwide exposure for books, which is particularly valuable for publishers of niche and backlist titles where an expensive marketing program isn't feasible, said Jennifer Grant, product marketing manager for Google Book Search. "That's really where Google and technology can come into play and help market these books very cost-efficiently...and help these books find their readers."

Publishers participating in Google Book Search can link to their titles on their own Web site within links such as:

**http://print.google.com/print?isbn=0123456789**

Be sure to replace the ISBN above (the digits following the equal sign) with the ISBN for your title. The only problem is, there's no guarantee the visitor who just left your site for Google will come back. If you're trying to get direct sales from your Web site, this could be an issue. At the Google Book Search site, your visitor will see **Buy** links to a variety of retailers, including Amazon.com, Barnes & Noble, BookSense, and of course Google Base, the search engine's product listing area.

## Accidental book discovery

One huge advantage for authors about Google Book Search is it enables people to discover your book, even if they weren't necessarily looking for a book. If a Google.com user searches for words that appear in your title or text, a link to your book can be displayed above the regular Web-page results. This can lead to dozens or hundreds more people stumbling onto your book daily.

Like Amazon's Search Inside program, Google Book Search gives free access to your book's complete table of contents and index. In response, savvy nonfiction publishers these days are printing tables of contents with as much detail as possible, making them more attractive to browsers. For example, instead of a brief table showing only chapter headings, the table mentions every section and subsection, nearly down to the paragraph level. The more information you can pack into your table of contents, the more likely you can hook a reader who's begun skimming it online. Content tables should read like a high-end restaurant menu, artfully mentioning every essential ingredient and whetting the reader's appetite.

Google runs small advertisements from its AdWords network on the Book Search pages, and splits the ad revenue with publishers. When someone clicks on an ad from a page displaying your book, you get paid, although publishers agree that revenue from the program has been minimal.

Safeguards are built into Google Book Search, similar to Amazon's Search Inside the Book. Users can view a limited number of pages of a low-resolution image of pages that can't be printed easily or saved. A portion of the book is kept offline so users wouldn't be able to see the whole book even if they had several different Google accounts.

A separate project, Google Library, is often confused with Google Book Search. The program is digitizing millions of books from six leading public and university library partners. The Library program has been controversial among many publishers because Google isn't asking for permission of rights holders before scanning the books.

## Instant Online Access

Google's first consumer bookselling initiative is called Instant Online Access. Consumers can purchase a perpetual license to view the entire contents of a book online. Publishers set the price for Instant Online Access, and Google keeps a 30 percent commission on sales.

Because selling online access to books might cannibalize sales of physical books, Google seems to be promising publishers that it will deliver more impulse purchases than brick-and-mortar bookstores. The program could promise better profit margins for publishers by freeing them from printing and distribution costs. For example, publishers keep as little as 30 percent of a paper book's cover price, with the rest split among bookstores, wholesalers, and distributors.

## Ad-Supported Access

Only 20 percent of a book's content normally is available for viewing in a given month on Google Book Search. However, publishers who are interested in publishing advertising-supported books can set the viewable percentage as high as they wish, all the way to 100 percent viewable. When publishers choose this Ad-Supported Access model, Google optimizes its ads for the book, trying to maximize revenue for the publisher. One publisher of travel books has enrolled all its titles in Ad-Supported Access on the theory that it won't hurt sales, while providing more chances that buyers will notice the books and decide to buy one.

Why would someone pay money for a book they can read for free on their computer monitor? A good percentage of travelers who are actually going on a trip to Italy, for example, will prefer to carry a pocket-sized travel book, and will likely buy one on impulse if they happen to see it. At least that's the theory.

Could it ever be possible for Internet publishers to earn more in advertising revenue from online viewership than in selling hard copies of their books? It's an intriguing idea, but it's unlikely we'll know the answer anytime soon. Google admits that ad payments to publishers have not been particularly strong.

## Google Print on Demand

Google knows that print-on-demand book publishing is an attractive option for small and niche publishers, so it's targeting publishers who don't already have digital copies of their books. With its POD program, Google will take the digital scan it makes when it enrolls a book into Google Book Search and make the file available to printers if the publisher opts for POD.

Google will create the digital file required for POD printers for free when it optically scans the book for inclusion in Google Book Search, and will host the file free.

To participate, publishers must have their own account with a POD printer and a relationship with an online retailer to handle fulfillment.

In late 2006, Google was considering plans for three additional bookselling programs:

- **Partial access**. Buyers would purchase access to only part of a book, such as a chapter – much like Amazon's Pages program.

- **Timed access**. Buyers would be able to purchase a one-day or weeklong license to view a book.

- **Digital file downloads.** Google believes downloadable books are inevitable, whenever an e-book viewing device is widely adopted by book readers, as Apple's iPod has drawn music lovers.

Publishers with questions or feedback can contact Google via e-mail at **Books-Support@google.com**.

## Windows Live Book Search

In 2006 Microsoft began building a rival book-search service. Although Microsoft's network has only a fraction of Google's search traffic today, things change quickly on the Internet.

Get more information at:

**www.Publisher.Live.com**

## Amazon Upgrade

Although Amazon has been selling downloadable e-books for years, in 2006 it added a new twist. Amazon Upgrade provides buyers with online access and searching of physical books they've already purchased. To upgrade their books, readers pay about 10 percent to 20 percent of the book's original price, and Amazon splits the revenue with publishers.

Amazon Upgrade is designed to appeal to buyers who want to receive a physical copy of the book, but are also willing to pay a bit extra for immediate online access and searching. Buyers view the book online through the Amazon Reader, the same interface used for Search Inside the Book. Amazon Upgrade users can print pages, but publishers can set the number of allowable printed pages.

Amazon users can view which previous purchases are available for Upgrade by browsing **Your Media Library**:

**http://amazon.com/gp/library**

Another place to view your list of upgradable books is:

**www.Amazon.com/gp/sitb/purchasing/booklist**

Amazon hopes Upgrade will appeal to publishers concerned that online access to books might cannibalize sales of physical books, cutting publisher revenue. With Upgrade, any purchases result in added revenue for publishers, since readers have already purchased the hard copy.

To be eligible to purchase upgrades, readers must buy the book directly from Amazon. Upgrades aren't available for books bought used or new from third-party Amazon vendors.

## Amazon's Mobipocket

In addition to Upgrade, which enables online viewing and searching, Amazon continues to sell e-books that readers can download. But in

2006 Amazon stopped selling Microsoft and Adobe-format books to focus on selling e-books through its wholly owned subsidiary, Mobipocket. The free Mobipocket Reader software allows users of PDA handheld computers to view e-books in the Mobipocket format.

Mobipocket books will also be sold through other online retailers. The promise, especially for self-published authors, is the potential to reach millions more readers at low cost.

Mobipocket, along with Amazon's BookSurge self-publishing unit, could enable Amazon to take a big share of the world's vanity-press business with little risk. Selling paid placement and other listing enhancements such as keyword visibility could provide a significant new revenue stream for Amazon.

Skeptics worry that Mobipocket could create a monopoly in the e-book marketplace if Amazon sells only Mobipocket books and the format becomes dominant. Traditional publishers are concerned that giving virtually free content-creation tools to millions of independent writers will undercut prices of all books.

To join Mobipocket, register at its publisher portal, eBookBase:

**www.Mobipocket.com/eBookBase/en/homepage/apply.asp?Type=Publisher**

Then register, print and sign Mobipocket's publisher agreement:

**www.Mobipocket.com/eBookBase/en/Homepage/pub_agreement.asp**

Fax in the agreement. After Amazon receives your signed publisher agreement, the Mobipocket team will notify you via e-mail of your account activation. Then you can log into eBookBase to start uploading and selling your e-books.

To convert your books to the Mobipocket format, you can download a free copy of the necessary software, Mobipocket Creator, Publisher Edition. You'll be able to upload directly from the Mobipocket Creator software or using the eBookBase Web interface:

**www.Mobipocket.com/eBookBase/en/Homepage/default.asp**

The e-books you've uploaded will be available through Amazon, Mobipocket.com, and other retailers. For a list of retailers who sell the books, see:

**www.Mobipocket.com/ebookbase/en/homepage/partners.asp?Type=Retailer**

For more information, join the mailing list of Amazon's Digital Text Team by sending an e-mail to **DigitalBooks@Amazon.com**.

## Amazon digital audio

Digital audiobooks are one of the fastest-growing book categories. Amazon has been developing a digital audiobook store and drafting its contract for publishers. As of late 2006, Amazon was still accepting audiobooks from publishers who wish to send them through postal mail on a CD or USB 2.0 drive.

Subscribe to announcements regarding this program by sending an e-mail to **Digital-Audio@Amazon.com**.

## Amazon Pages

Amazon Pages sells pay-per-view access to small portions of books, down to the chapter, section or even page level. Publishers set the price and Amazon splits the revenue.

Publishers interested in participating can get more information by sending an e-mail to at **DigitalBooks@Amazon.com**.

# Book promotion with e-books

So far, electronic books, or e-books, haven't gotten much traction with consumers. Until an excellent, inexpensive reader gadget becomes available, e-book sales probably won't be significant. In the meantime, though, e-books and downloadable excerpts are a good way to generate awareness of your book and to distribute spinoff products like special reports.

## Amazon Shorts

Authors can use Amazon Shorts as a vehicle for publicizing new books or promoting backlist titles. Readers pay 49 cents to download the Short in plain text or PDF format.

For example, historian David McCullough used an Amazon Short to build awareness of his 2006 hardcover *1776*. His Short was a 1,700-word essay titled "Faces" on how Revolutionary War leaders are perceived today. The Short included links to *1776* and nine previous McCullough works sold on Amazon.

Each Amazon Short includes an author biography and photograph, and links to their other books sold on Amazon. Shorts are a good way for readers to try new authors because the low price encourages reader experimentation and impulse buying.

Some authors have used Shorts to serialize works, or to update readers with extensions of their books, or an entirely new story with familiar characters.

Some nonfiction authors have used Shorts to generate new customers for other products. In one longtime bestselling Short, *Why Authors Are Cranky*, author Bruce Holland Rogers promotes his own Web site, where readers can purchase a one-year e-mail subscription to Rogers' short stories for $10. The Web link in Rogers' Amazon Short is live, so readers can click right to the site:

**www.ShortShortShort.com**.

## Client acquisition

One of the most prolific Amazon Shorts authors is business consultant Lonnie Pacelli, who has 15 bestselling Shorts. His Shorts are cross-promotional tools for his two business hardcovers and 13 full-length downloadable e-books sold on Amazon for $4.99 each. All these e-books help promote fee-based seminars Pacelli conducts on his Web site. His most popular Amazon Short is *The Perfect Brainstorm*.

Shorts can be used to test ideas for full-length books or expanding into new topics or genres. Authors can use Shorts as full-blown laboratories, testing story concepts and soliciting reader feedback. For example, fiction writers can update characters from a book series, giving hints on what might happen in the next hardcover installment, with readers serving as a focus group.

You can browse and search all Amazon Shorts here:

**www.Amazon.com/Shorts**.

Some other interesting work with Amazon Shorts:

- In *A Man and His Luggage*, Stuart Woods departs from his tried-and-true mystery genre for a humorous essay on how to find the perfect travel companion.

- In his Short *Bubble After Bubble in the Ongoing Bubble Boom*, Harry S. Dent updates his 2004 economics bestselling hardcover *The Next Great Bubble Boom*. Six months later, his publisher issued an updated edition of the hardcover.

Amazon recommends a length of 2,000 to 10,000 words for Shorts, and requires they be exclusive to Amazon for the first six months. Publishers keep 60 percent of the revenue, while Amazon covers the cost of payment collection and customer service.

There's no copy protection for Amazon Shorts; the text or PDFs can be printed, copied, and forwarded via e-mail. When viewed as an HTML document, the text can be copied and pasted into a word processor.

To apply for participation in the Amazon Shorts program, send an e-mail to **Amazon-Shorts@Amazon.com**. To be eligible, you must have at least one book currently for sale on Amazon.

## Selling e-books on your site

Self-publishers are free to sell their book as a PDF document from their own Web site. You can also add spin-off reports, or perhaps even compile your blog posts into a booklet.

Selling downloadable text files or PDF documents and collecting payments with PayPal or a credit-card merchant account is one option. You can further automate the process by using one of these services:

- **www.ClickBank.com**, which collects payments, hosts your file, and enables affiliates to resell your e-book if you wish.
- **www.Payloadz.com** automates payments and downloads, allowing you to sell e-books on your site, eBay or through affiliates, and to accept payment through PayPal or Google Checkout.

# Syndicating your content

"Information wants to be free," as the saying goes. Yet it's also true that the best way to sell information is by giving some away free. You can apply this to fiction, and particularly to nonfiction, where every bit of exposure helps build your reputation.

Most people don't purchase a book the first time they hear of it, but the sixth or seventh time they're exposed to it. The more frequently you can pop up in front of your potential audience—providing valuable, free content—the larger your audience becomes. When Internet searchers discover valuable content, they become prime candidates for buying a book from someone regarded as an expert.

The benefits of posting free sample content online grow by the day. Not only can consumers find you, but reporters and news producers increasingly turn to the Internet to find expert sources and story ideas. This can lead to exposure and credibility that can't be bought at any price.

Here are some good ways of providing sample content to burnish your reputation and achieve expert status:

- **Post question-and-answer content.** On your blog or Web site, summarize the best questions you receive from readers via e-mail, phone calls, letters or personal conversations. Publish them in a question-and-answer format. This provides interesting, valuable, and easy-to-read content. Q&A content is simple to produce, especially if you're already producing the raw material by answering e-mails. When you post this content publicly, your entire audience benefits, instead of just one person (although you should omit personally identifying information where appropriate). Further, Q&As expand your audience because the format boosts your visibility with search engines. Many people searching the Web actually type questions into Google, such as "How to stop thumb-sucking." You can rewrite the questions for clarity, or even write the question yourself to help illustrate a point. You can use this same type of content to build an FAQ, or Frequently Asked Questions, page on your site.

- **Offer book excerpts or sample chapters.** Make this available as a PDF download from your Web site. At a minimum, you should offer your book's table of contents, index, and a short excerpt. If you have a copy of your book in a word-processing file, you can convert sections into PDF documents with free software from the site **www.PDF995.com**.

One popular science-fiction author, Cory Doctorow, provides free downloads of the entire text of all his novels at his site, **www.CrapHound.com**. The resulting publicity far outweighs the cost of any lost book sales, Doctorow says: "It's about word of mouth. My readers have large social circles of friends whom they never see face-to-face."

- **Participate in online discussions.** Answering queries about your topic on discussion boards and e-mail lists can lure more visitors to your site. Find relevant groups on Web boards and in groups sponsored by Yahoo, MSN, LiveJournal, and America Online. Add a three- or four-line signature to the bottom of your posts, including your Web address and current book title. Be sure to provide helpful information; don't post purely promotional messages. Follow the rules of the group, which sometimes preclude commercial content.

- **Post comments on blogs related to your topic.** Most blogs allow you to include a link back to your site in your comment. Invest the time in providing useful, thoughtful commentary, and you'll bring some new visitors to your site.

## Article banks

An increasingly popular way to get exposure for your book is by contributing to online article banks. One of the most popular, **EzineArticles.com**, has more than 40,000 participating authors. Contributors aren't paid, but they figure the added exposure is worth the effort.

If your articles are accepted, they're featured on EzineArticles.com and made available for reuse on other Web sites, blogs and e-mail newsletters. Each article includes a “resource box” with links back to your site.

Although article syndication can provide great exposure, be selective about the content you contribute. Don’t offer any content that appears on your site without first rewriting it. Search engines such as Google constantly filter out “duplicate content” from search results. If an article from your site appears elsewhere on the Internet, one of the Web pages probably will be deleted from search results, and chances are it will be yours. Search-engine experts call this the *duplicate content penalty*.

## How duplicate content backfires

Let’s imagine you’ve written a book about pottery, and to promote it, you publish a pottery blog. Last year on your blog, you wrote a nifty tutorial on fixing broken pottery. Word has gotten around, and now every pottery site on the Internet links to your pottery-repair page. Because of all these links, your page is the top Google result for “repairing pottery,” “fixing pottery,” and several related queries. That single page is your Web site’s crown jewel, accounting for half your new visitors and a good portion of your book sales.

Now let’s imagine you try to squeeze even *more* traffic from your pottery-repair article. You post it to EzineArticles.com, without changing much except to add the links back to your site. Meanwhile, you upload the same article to other syndication sites like GoArticles.com and IdeaMarketers.com.

Now you sit back and wait for the extra traffic, but the exact opposite happens—you see less traffic, not more. Now that your article appears on a bigger, more popular site, it’s likely that Google will send searchers there instead of sending them to your site. Google has made a quick calculation of which site is more authoritative, and because EzineArticles.com has more links than your site, it wins. Google doesn’t care that you wrote the article and have the Internet’s best pottery site.

The lesson is, keep your most valuable content on your site exclusively. And if you’re going to syndicate existing content, rewrite it substantially so the search engines don’t penalize you for it.

Google’s Adam Lasnik, the company’s “search evangelist,” offers two tips for avoiding the duplicate content penalty:

- If you syndicate an article containing the same or very similar language that appears somewhere on your site, ensure the syndicated article includes a link back to the original article on your site. Don't include only a link to your home page or some other page.

- Minimize boilerplate language on all your content. For example, instead of including lengthy copyright notices at the bottom of all your Web pages, include a brief summary with a link to a page containing your full copyright notice.

None of these safeguards, however, is foolproof. The only sure way to avoid the duplicate content penalty is by syndicating original material only, and keeping your best material exclusive to your site.

## Really Simple Syndication

**RSS**, or Really Simple Syndication, is a Web feed that allows people to view summaries of your blog posts. Readers are automatically notified when you post new material. Most blogging software automatically publishes an RSS feed for you, or you can open a free account with Feedburner, which will publish an RSS feed for you with several enhancements:

**www.Feedburner.com**

Although an RSS feed makes your blog more visible, there are also a few disadvantages. For example, readers who can view all your blog content within an RSS reader may quit visiting your Web site, and won't be exposed to other types of content. You can minimize this problem by syndicating a brief summary of your blog posts, perhaps the first 100 words. Readers who want to continue would need to click through to your site.

## BlogBurst

BlogBurst syndicates content from member blogs to the Web sites of metro newspapers like the San Francisco Chronicle, Washington Post, the Austin American-Statesman, and Gannett papers. BlogBurst functions as a wire service, providing the newspaper sites with a rich variety of niche blog content, while giving the blogs wider exposure.

When a reader at the newspaper site clicks on a blog headline, BlogBurst displays the blog post along with advertising. Ad revenue is split with the blogger and the newspaper.

BlogBurst participants must publish their entire blog posts in their RSS feed, not just summaries. The content must be family-friendly, and updated at least once a week.

To enroll, see:

**www.BlogBurst.com/blogger/add-blog.html**

## Traditional media interviews

Landing national media exposure can greatly enhance your book sales, but many new authors don't have the resources to hire a publicist. One way to get exposure in newspapers, radio and television without hiring a publicist is **www.PRLeads.com**. Several times a day, users receive a list of queries from journalists looking for expert sources for the stories they're writing.

On a typical day, a PRLeads subscriber might see a query like this:

> SUBJECT:
> BUSINESS : Small Companies Going into International Markets – Boston Daily News
>
> For a national newspaper, I'm writing a story on how small-business owners should make the decision to go into international markets. What factors should they consider? How can they evaluate the opportunity? How soon after establishing yourself domestically should you consider this? I'm looking for comments from experts, and examples of entrepreneurs who have been dealing with this issue.

Authors and experts with relevant expertise could send this reporter a brief e-mail, describing their credentials and how they can address the topic. Later the reporter might follow up via phone or e-mail for an interview. Subscriptions to PRLeads cost $99 a month. For more information, see:

**www.PRLeads.com/pr-leads-faq.htm**

# Press releases

Not too long ago, press releases were terribly expensive because they had to be mailed—or faxed or wire-delivered—to traditional media outlets like newspapers. Then your message would reach a gatekeeper, like an editor, who might decide to trash your release. If your release were used at all, the final article could be totally different from your intended message, and your name or book title might not even appear.

Now dozens of inexpensive and free press-release distribution services can make your announcement visible to the entire world, exactly as you wrote it. For an additional fee of about $40, these services will post your news to sites like Google News, Yahoo News, and others, providing even wider exposure.

When writing a press release, the most important thing is to focus on the *reader*, not on you and your book. What problem does your book solve for the reader, or what kind of entertainment does it provide? Nobody wants to read an announcement that simply says Mrs. Y wrote a book about Topic X. Who cares? Tell your audience *what's in it for them.*

Here's an effective (but fictionalized) book press release that generates interest by focusing on readers:

> American parents are furious with Hollywood for glamorizing stick-thin bodies, and many girls say they're self-conscious about their bodies as a result of movies, television and magazines. This national obsession with thinness is resulting in eating disorders and depression among millions of teens, according to Anita Jones, author of Nourishing Girls: Help Your Teen Develop Self-Esteem and a Healthy Body Image....

And here's the other side of the coin, a release that induces boredom by focusing solely on the author and his world:

> In a newly released political thriller, ex-diplomat, military intelligence officer, college football standout and news reporter James McNeil authentically captures the hardball maneuverings and virtual mortality of Washington power politics. Critics give two thumbs up to Shotgun Diplomacy, the author's second novel....

For tips on writing effective press releases, see:

**www.PRWeb.com/pressreleasetips.php**

**www.eMediaWire.com** is a popular channel of press release distribution for many authors and publishers announcing new titles.

Here are a few other popular press release distribution services:

**www.PRNewswire.com**
**www.Send2Press.com**
**www.PRLeap.com**
**www.eReleases.com**
**www.BusinessWire.com**

## Protecting your content

The Internet is a great publicity vehicle because it makes your content freely available. By the same token, the openness of the Web makes it easy for people to steal your work. An unscrupulous blogger or Webmaster can copy and paste your most valuable material onto his site within minutes without asking permission.

Every month or so, you should search the Web for some of the text from several of your pages. A Google search for a string of six to eight words within quotation marks should turn up any sites that have copied your content.

A stern message to the owner of the site—or, failing that, the company that hosts the site—usually results in deletion of the stolen material. Here's an example of a cease-and-desist notice you can send via e-mail:

> Dear John Doe,
>
> It's come to my attention that you are republishing my original content from MySite.com on your Web site, YourSite.com. For example, page [ADDRESS] on your site includes the following paragraphs: [TEXT].
>
> Your unauthorized use of my original material violates U.S. and international copyright laws. If the offending material remains available on your site 72 hours from now, I will have no choice but to pursue legal action against you.
>
> Please comply with my request, so that we can remedy this situation without unnecessary difficulty.
>
> Sincerely,
>
> Jane Doe
> MySite.com

If no contact information appears on the offending Web site, enter the site's domain name in the search box at:

**www.Register.com/retail/whois.rcmx**

This will return the name and contact information of the person or company who registered the domain or the site's hosting company. Also try sending your message to webmaster@[domain name] and abuse@[domain name].

Another source of contact information for Web sites is:

**www.DomainTools.com**

# Beyond the blogosphere

Because of their interactive features and visibility on the Web, blogs have largely replaced other book-publicity vehicles. Just a few years ago, "chat" sessions on proprietary services like America Online were a prime target of book publicists. Although the audiences for many of those proprietary services are now splintered across the Web, a whole world of opportunity remains outside the blogosphere.

Popular Web sites devoted to a certain topic or book genre often have a lively discussion board. The best way to find these discussion groups is to search Google for the types of questions your audience tends to ask most frequently. Once you've found them, contribute to the conversation, but don't blatantly advertise your book. Include a discreet signature at the bottom of your posts, three or four lines of text listing your Web site, contact information, and buy-the-book links.

## BookCrossing

Book clubs and discussion groups have always been a great word-of-mouth generator, and the Internet has given them global reach. BookCrossing.com is a virtual book club whose members pass along books they've enjoyed. Members can recommend books at the Web site and ask to receive books via postal mail. Another pass-along technique is for members to "accidentally" leave books at bus stops, dentist offices and other places, along with a sticker inviting whoever finds the book to join BookCrossing—a practice members call "releasing books into the wild."

Launched in 2001, BookCrossing now has about 520,000 members circulating 3.5 million books. Membership is free, and the group has grown primarily from word of mouth, not advertising. At first, founder Ron Hornbaker feared authors would oppose BookCrossing and brand it the book world's "Napster," referring to the online music-sharing service accused of copyright infringement. But hundreds of authors have discovered that BookCrossing can generate strong word of mouth for their book, Hornbaker says. Active members discover many new authors and purchase lots of books based on member recommendations.

BookCrossing remains unpopular with some authors, who argue that access to free copies of books deprives them of income. Perhaps these are the same authors who would rather not see their work on the shelves of public libraries—another strong word-of-mouth generator, in the opinion of many successful authors.

Many authors say exposure through BookCrossing generates more buzz and sales than mailing review copies to magazines and newspapers. Although there is nothing wrong with authors donating their own books to BookCrossing, Hornbaker cautions that authors should be transparent about their activities, and identify themselves as a book's author. In no circumstance should authors post a message on BookCrossing's discussion boards or send a private message promoting the author's book.

## Usenet, Google groups

There are nearly 40,000 Usenet newsgroups, which are bulletin-board style forums about every conceivable topic. Usage of newsgroups has declined in recent years as blogs and niche Web sites have gained readers. Although some Usenet groups have become riddled with spam and irrelevant messages, some useful, widely read groups remain.

A few years ago, special software was required to view or post to Usenet discussions. This is no longer necessary; Google now hosts these groups on an easy-to-use Web interface, calling them Google Groups, at:

**www.Groups.Google.com**

To find groups in your topic, type some terms into the search box at the top of the Google Groups page. You can also browse the list of group categories.

Most newsgroups are unmoderated, and you can post messages immediately. Other newsgroups are moderated, and require posters to e-mail their message to a moderator for approval. Moderated newsgroups have charters outlining prescribed conduct and whether any commercial-related messages are permitted.

When you submit a post to a moderated group, the moderator must first approve your message before it appears on Google Groups and the rest of Usenet. If you post the same message in multiple groups and one of the groups is moderated, the message will be sent only to the moderator of the moderated group. Then the moderator will decide if your post should be approved to appear on all the groups.

## Yahoo, AOL Groups

Yahoo hosts thousands of active discussion groups. You can browse by category at **http://Groups.Yahoo.com**, or search with keywords. After joining the group, you can view messages on the Web or subscribe via e-mail.

America Online hosts many special-interest groups, but use has been declining as the network's membership has sagged in recent years. AOL no longer requires a paid membership for users of groups. See:

**http://Groups.AOL.com**

## Getting buzz on eBay

Another place where authors can expose their book to millions more potential buyers is eBay, the auction Web site. eBay has millions of book buyers constantly browsing the site for new, interesting items.

One of eBay's weaknesses in bookselling relative to Amazon is that it provides few product recommendations or reviews. Still, eBay can be a useful tool for raising awareness of your title, even if it doesn't result in a substantial amount of sales on eBay itself.

One particularly effective tactic is to periodically auction a single copy of your book for sale in one or more relevant subject categories. Buyers who are interested in your book but don't want to wait until the end of the auction will look for a copy elsewhere for immediate purchase.

Here are some tips for getting the maximum number of lookers on eBay:

- Start your auction at 1 cent. That will attract early and frequent bidding, which creates more interest. Some eBay users scan for only those items with several bids already, on the theory that frequent bidding is a sign of an interesting or unique find. You can also sell your book at a fixed price on eBay, but auctions attract more eyeballs.

- Extend your auction to 10 days, instead of the usual seven-day auction. You'll get more lookers and bids for a nominal fee. The extra three days allows bidding to rise and gives impatient buyers an incentive to purchase immediately somewhere else.

- Mention the ISBN at least twice in your auction description so impatient browsers and losing bidders can buy elsewhere. Use every possible keyword in your description. A small excerpt from the introduction can drive visitors to your listing. It's not necessary to limit your description to the back cover copy.

- Try a **Featured Plus** listing to get more exposure. The extra fee is $20, but can be offset by the final bidding price, increased sales outside eBay, and word of mouth.

- Include a link from your auction listing to a page on your Web site where readers can download your table of contents, introduction and sample pages.

- List your book under multiple categories on eBay, not just "books." Let's imagine your book is about doll making. You could list under **nonfiction books**, **collectibles**, **toys**, **hobbies**, and perhaps five other related categories. You'll pay additional listing fees, but gain exposure among people interested in your topic, but not necessarily searching for a book about it.

Another tactic for eBay selling is to differentiate the book listing from what's available from Amazon and other retailers. You could sell autographed copies of your book, in eBay's "collectible" book category or in the book's subject area. You could also develop a package deal, selling your book with a bonus pamphlet or report.

## eBay Stores

An eBay Store can be worth the basic fee of $15.95 even if you're a self-publisher with a single title. Having a store allows you to sell copies of your book at a fixed price, and you can offer discounts on slightly damaged or shopworn books.

Your eBay Store listing will also be indexed by Google and other search engines, giving your title more visibility on the Web.

Another benefit of having an eBay Store is you can link from your Store to your Web site or blog. This not only provides extra traffic to your site, but the link from eBay enhances your site's ranking with search engines.

# Revenue from your Web site

A steady audience on your Web site provides additional income opportunities through affiliate programs and advertising. If your site becomes extremely popular, the revenue could rival your income from book sales.

Some bloggers report that a combination of affiliate and advertising revenue can result in about 1.5 cents of income for each unique daily visitor to your site. At that rate, a site averaging 1,500 unique daily visitors can generate about $8,200 in annual revenue—not bad for something that requires no ongoing work on your part. Depending on your audience and the type of products related to your book, you might do better or worse.

New sites usually generate negligible revenue, but advertising or affiliate programs can still be worthwhile. Your audience may appreciate niche advertising, and these programs can boost your visibility with search engines. One option is to donate your affiliate and ad revenues to charities admired by your audience, which sometimes can be handled automatically. The public-relations benefit of donating could outweigh the monetary value, and you won't have to account for it as income and pay tax on it.

In any case, advertising shouldn't overly distract visitors from the main purpose of your site—generating awareness of your book.

Here are some of the leading advertising and affiliate programs authors can use on their Web sites:

## Amazon Associates program

Amazon's affiliate program is called Amazon Associates. You can display links for your book and related books and products on Amazon, and when your visitors click through to Amazon and make a purchase, you're paid a commission. Typically you'll receive about 6 percent, so the sale of a $20 book yields a $1.20 referral fee.

Amazon Associates is one of the most familiar and successful programs on the Internet, with more than 1 million member sites. After joining you receive an Associates ID code, which you insert into your links to Amazon products.

Under Amazon Associates' performance-based compensation plan, affiliates earn referral fees ranging from 4 percent to 8.5 percent, depending on volume. For a site referring 21 or more affiliate sales during a quarterly period, Amazon awards 6 percent, payable at the end of the quarter. You can collect your fees in the form of a check, direct deposit, or an Amazon gift certificate.

Besides providing Amazon Associates links to specific books, you can display Amazon banner ads or search boxes on your site, and you'll earn referral fees on sales resulting from those clicks.

After your visitors click on your Associates link, you'll receive commissions not only on book purchases, but most other purchases those customers make during the following 24 hours. For example, if your visitor buys a plasma TV, you'll get a commission on that.

In 2006 Amazon Associates introduced a new contextual program called Omakase, which displays different products based on the content on your site and your visitor's browsing history at Amazon. The advantage for affiliates is that Omakase is dynamic, exposing your audience to different books each time they visit a different page on your site, increasing the odds of a purchase.

The name Omakase is Japanese for "Leave it up to us," a custom in Japanese restaurants in which the chef improvises a meal based on his knowledge of the diner's preferences.

For more information, visit:

**www.Amazon.com/Associates**

## Barnes & Noble

Barnes & Noble's affiliate program isn't as widely used as Amazon's but it can attract buyers who prefer Barnes & Noble, particularly members of its loyalty program. Members receive an additional 10 percent discount on purchases. See:

**www.bn.com/affiliate**

## Commission Junction

Opening an account at Commission Junction provides access to hundreds of niche affiliate programs. You'll find affiliate opportunities for nearly any type of product, including dozens of specialized book retailers. The site provides the codes you'll need to insert on your Web site, and consolidated reports of your commissions. See:

**www.CommissionJunction.com**

## eBay

If there's a category on eBay of interest to your target niche, it may be well worth the effort of opening an affiliate account. You can display relevant ads for popular auctions on your site. The ads contain product information, gallery images, bidding prices, and ending times. eBay claims that the click-through rates for these ads are double that of regular banner ads. After joining, you can operate your eBay affiliate account using a network like Commission Junction, mentioned above.

For more information, see:

**http://affiliates.ebay.com**

## Google AdSense, other advertising

Google's AdSense program is perhaps the best-known Web ad network, and it's relatively easy to sign up and incorporate text or banner ads onto your site. For more information, see:

**www.Google.com/Adsense**

Two alternatives to AdSense are **www.AdBrite.com** and **www.BlogAds.com**.

# Pay-per-click advertising

Pay-per-click advertising has revolutionized online promotion, and has been wonderfully effective for many Internet businesses. The prime advantage of pay-per-click is its ability to deliver your ad to targeted audiences. Unfortunately, like other forms of advertising, pay-per-click is seldom a cost-effective technique for marketing books.

Although pay-per-click can bring targeted traffic to your site, it's unlikely you'll convert enough of those visitors into buyers to make your ad campaign worthwhile. Google, for example, will charge you 75 cents or more per click for competitive keywords, and only a small fraction of those clicks will result in sales. Even if you're paying as little as 10 cents per click, your advertising bill will likely exceed the revenue from sales, in the experience of many publishers. With typical consumer books, there's just not enough profit margin to pay for the ads.

## Google AdWords

With AdWords, advertisers write short three-line text ads, then bid on keywords relevant to their ad. The ads appear alongside relevant search results or on content pages. For example, to advertise a book about tropical fish, you might bid on several different keywords and phrases—**aquarium**, **exotic fish**, **fishkeeping**, and **pet fish**. Depending on how popular those words and phrases are with other advertisers, you might have to pay a minimum of 10 cents, 30 cents, or several dollars for each click. The higher your bid, the higher your ad shows up on the relevant page.

Although most general-interest books can't be cost-effectively marketed using AdWords, the program can be effective for specialty publishers and sellers of certain high-margin products, such as:

- Expensive books such as technical and professional manuals costing more than $75, where a built-in advertising budget of more than $15 per unit can be justified.

- Publishers with a long line of complementary books and products. If customers spend a lifetime average of $100 or more on your products, acquiring new customers with AdWords might work.

- Business consultants or professional speakers, whose books help establish their reputation and help attract clients, speaking engagements, or seminar attendees.

Learn more about Google's AdWords program at:

**www.Google.com/Adwords/Learningcenter**

## Yahoo Search Marketing

The main competitor to AdWords is Yahoo Search Marketing. In recent years, Yahoo's program has lagged Google's AdWords in effectiveness and ease of use, but recently Yahoo has been working to improve its program.

For more information:

**http://SearchMarketing.Yahoo.com**.

# Power tools

One of the favorite pastimes of authors is checking the Amazon Sales Ranks of their books. In the past few years, several free tools have emerged to help authors and publishers monitor the ranks of their books and competing titles.

**www.RankForest.com** allows you to chart your Amazon Sales Rank by drawing a line graph similar to a stock chart. You can add books to a "collection" for quick reference, and leave comments on books. Many of the site's features are free.

**www.TicTap.com** also allows you to track Amazon Sales Ranks over time on a bar graph and compare purchase prices from different retailers.

## Amazon Sales Rank

Amazon ranks each book based on how often it sells relative to every other book in its catalog of some 3.5 million titles. The best-selling book is ranked 1; the slowest seller exceeds 3,500,000. Books for which Amazon hasn't recorded a sale are ranked "None."

A book's Amazon Sales Rank appears in the **Product Details** section of its detail page on Amazon. Sales ranks are recalculated hourly, and can change significantly day to day.

Since Amazon has an estimated 70 percent market share among Internet book retailers, its sales rankings are the best free, publicly available information about the relative sales performance of individual titles. The rankings include new and used books sold by third-party sellers on Amazon's Marketplace platform.

Amazon doesn't publicly discuss its sales figures for individual titles, so it's impossible to correlate the rankings with quantity of sales. However, based on anecdotal reports from various publishers, you can assume that an Amazon sales rank of 5,000 translates into about 15 to 20 sales per day, depending on seasonal factors.

## TitleZ

**www.TitleZ.com** allows users to instantly retrieve historic and current Amazon rankings and create printable reports with 7-day, 30-day, 90-day, and lifetime averages. This allows you to see how book topic areas or individual titles perform over time relative to others.

TitleZ is a handy tool for evaluating book topic ideas because you can gauge the potential audience for a given topic or title. Using TitleZ you can easily assemble a list of related books with their historical sales rankings and descriptions. This indicates whether other books on the topic have succeeded or failed, and may show where opportunities exist or where markets are saturated.

TitleZ also provides pricing information on competitive titles, helping you determine the right price for your book. You can also track your book's performance over time to assess the effect of promotional efforts and marketing programs.

## Affiliate partnerships

Once your book achieves a modest Amazon Sales Rank, you'll have clout outside Amazon too. For example, you can pursue affiliate sales on Web sites that feature content related to your book. Many sites are affiliates of Amazon or BarnesAndNoble.com and have a "Bookshelf" page. Here's an example of a bookshelf page, with affiliate links to books in the column on the right:

**www.WineLoversPage.com/winebook/quickbooks.phtml**

If your book about wine was featured here, you'd undoubtedly get extra book sales from visitors who noticed the link to your book on Amazon. Likewise, the owner of this Web site would be pleased to feature your book here because he or she would be raking in more affiliate commissions on sales of your book. So don't sit back and hope that the site owner discovers your book and adds it to the Bookshelf page—suggest it yourself. Point out that your book fits perfectly with the content of the site and will generate strong affiliate revenue based on its Amazon Sales Rank.

How can you find sites like this to feature your book? As an example, we'll use our imaginary title *How to Grow Organic Strawberries*:

- Go to Google's "Advanced Search" page, **www.Google.com/advanced_search**
- In the box labeled **with all of the words**, enter this text, including the quotation marks: "In association with Amazon.com", bookstore, strawberries.
- Scroll down to the section labeled **Domain,** and change the pull-down window from **only** to **don't**. In the blank on the right, enter **Amazon.com.**
- Click the gray button on the top right, "Google Search."

The results will include Amazon affiliate sites with content pertaining to our book keyword "strawberries."

We might be able to find more relevant sites by tweaking our search. Instead of using only the keyword "strawberries," we'll try these combinations:

- Organic strawberries
- Growing strawberries
- Strawberry growing
- Organic gardening
- Healthy food

Some of the sites Google returns may not be book affiliate sites, or might be inappropriate for other reasons. For the rest, you might contact the Web site owner via e-mail or via telephone from contact information from the site. If there's no contact information listed, there's often a Webmaster e-mail address near the bottom of home pages. Sometimes a site's "advertise with us" link will provide the fastest response, but you won't be offering to pay for advertising.

A personal note to the Web site owner works best. Explain who you are and why you think the site's visitors will appreciate learning about your book.

Driving more sales to Amazon through its affiliates will further boost your sales rank and continue the positive feedback loop, with more people discovering your book, and adding more weight for your title in Amazon's recommendations and search results.

## Analyzing your traffic

Part of creating a useful, valuable Web site is understanding the behavior of your visitors—how they find your site, and what they do once they arrive. Depending on which Web host you've selected, you'll have access to some type of traffic reports that can provide valuable insight into which of your content pages are most effective.

If you're doing any paid advertising, these reports can also help you figure out whether your ads are effective. Google Analytics is a very good free tool that provides detailed statistics about the activity of your visitors, and it's fairly easy to add the service to your site. For more information:

**www.Google.com/Analytics**

**www.MyBlogLog.com** is a handy tool for bloggers who want quick statistics on where their visitors are coming from, and what blog posts they click on most often.

**www.StatCounter.com** and **www.SiteMeter.com** are other free resources for tracking visitor activity at your site.

## Linking strategy

Many bloggers publish a list of links to related blogs on their sidebar, known as a *blogroll*. This can be helpful for your visitors, but it can be overdone. You should strike a balance between giving your visitors easy access to useful, outside information, while not encouraging them to leave your site sooner than they otherwise might.

It's counterproductive to link to marginally related sites from your home page because it dilutes your site's "authority" in Google rankings. A better solution is to link to outside content from within individual blog posts when relevant. Build a separate "resources" page on your site where you can point visitors to outside resources without getting penalized for it on your home page.

## Search engine optimization

The beauty of publishing a blog is that it naturally optimizes your content for indexing by search engines. A blog makes you highly visible, without your having to think too much about technique. Even so, it helps to know some basics of search engine optimization (SEO) to enhance your site's ability to draw new visitors.

The leading search engines are Google, Yahoo, and MSN.com. If your site doesn't already appear in search results, request that your site be added. To request indexing by the search engines, go to:

- Google: **http://Google.com/addurl.html**
- MSN: **http://Search.MSN.com/docs/submit.aspx**
- Yahoo: **http://Search.Yahoo.com/info/submit.html**

Another way to get your site included in the search engines is to have at least one incoming link from another site that's already been indexed by search engines. The next time Google and other search engines crawl the other site, they'll follow the link to yours.

The essential ingredients for a high-ranking site change periodically. Many bloggers and Webmasters waste time and money chasing the "perfect" formula for getting to the top of search results, and then must start over when Google changes the way it evaluates Web pages. Rather than spending lots of time trying to game the system, you can better spend your time adding valuable content to your site.

## Keyword density

One effective way to make your content more visible with search engines is *keyword density*. Let's imagine you're writing a blog post about how to wax a car in 30 minutes. You might write the title: "Waxing your car in less than 30 minutes: Here's how." This way, the most important words, *waxing* and *car*, appear at the beginning of the title. Your first sentence might be, "Waxing your car can be a time-consuming chore, but here's how to get it done fast." This reinforces your keywords. Repeating them again will enhance your keyword density and ensure your post ranks high in searches for those keywords.

Be consistent with word choices to maintain keyword density. Let's imagine you have a page on your site devoted to antique Ford

Thunderbird cars. Naturally, you'll want *Thunderbird* to appear several times on the page to rank high in search results for that keyword. So you'll want to keep using the word *Thunderbird* instead of slang or nicknames. The sentence "The 1969 *'Bird* was a stylish car" would dilute your keyword density.

Although keyword density makes it easier for your target audience to find you, don't overdo it. If you artificially jam the same keyword several times in each sentence, search engines will detect this and penalize you for "keyword stuffing."

Another way to get penalized with search engines is by participating in so-called "link farms." These are sites that trade or sell Web links, but it seldom works. The only links that will truly boost your site are from high-ranking sites with content similar to yours. So forget about buying links to boost your SEO. Simply produce good content for your audience, and the links and traffic will come naturally.

You've probably seen advertisements for consultants who promise to make your site No. 1 in the search engines within 30 days. Don't waste your money. Chances are, anyone who makes such promises is incompetent, a charlatan, or both.

Your most important links will be from sites in your niche. Links from crowded social sites like MySpace or discussion boards won't strengthen your site's rankings much, says Dave Taylor, author of *Growing Your Business with Google*. "Theoretically all links are good, but I don't believe that links from jungles like MySpace are going to give you any real boost," Taylor says. "Those sites that are easy to get links from just aren't going to have the value of, say, a link from the home page of Stanford.edu or Wiley.com."

Google provides an excellent tutorial for optimizing your Web site:

**www.Google.com/Support/Webmasters**

## The length of your lease

Many factors influencing how much juice your Web site has are outside your immediate control. For example, if your domain is new—registered within the previous year—it will get short shrift in search results. Some experts call this the *Google sandbox effect*, meaning that new Web sites are given a probationary period.

Why would Google penalize new blogs and Web sites? Isn't a new blogger or Webmaster just as capable of producing valuable content? The answer is, newcomers are penalized to help the search engines deal with spam Web sites, a growing problem. Fly-by-night companies build spam sites using stolen content or machine-generated lists of keywords. The spammers sprinkle their sites with Google advertising and make a bit of money, at least until Google wises up and cuts off its ads. To limit their costs, the spammers register their domain for the minimum, one year—they don't want to pay in advance for a site they'll be abandoning soon. Google limits the traffic it sends to new sites to avoid helping these spammers make even more money.

How can you turn this to your advantage? By letting Google and the other search engines know your site isn't spam. Extend your domain registration several years into the future, instead of paying the one-year minimum. By paying your domain registration fees nine years in advance, you'll spend about $90 instead of the minimum $9 for one year. But the $90 investment can provide a big return. Bloggers and Webmasters report huge increases in search-engine traffic just weeks after extending their domain registration for multiple years, according to anecdotal reports.

## Publishers Portal

Designed for independent publishers, this service provided by Dial-A-Book, Inc. displays chapter excerpts of your book in more than 1,000 library online public access catalogs and on these Web sites used by readers and book dealers:

- Baker & Taylor, Title Source III
- Barnes & Noble.com
- Bowker, Books-in-Print Online
- Bowker, Syndetics
- Buy.com
- EBSCO, NoveList/NextReads
- Ingram, iPage
- On-line Computer Center, WorldCat/FirstSearch

Publishers Portal costs $25 per book, and participating titles are added to Dial-A-Book's Chapter One database. To participate, send an e-mail to info@publishersportal.com or visit:

**www.PublishersPortal.com**

## Privacy policies

If you collect data from your Web site visitors, consider posting a disclaimer. Privacy policies explain how names, addresses, and other information is used or shared with third parties.

The Better Business Bureau provides this suggested outline for privacy policies:

**www.bbbonline.org/privacy/sample_privacy.asp**

## Web site cardinal sins

Here are some of the most common ways author sites can be counterproductive:

• **Insisting the customer buy on your site.** Your site generates awareness of your book. The customer decides how to buy. You can make a suggestion, but if your goal is to sell as many books as possible, offer every buying option possible.

Sure, your profit margin may be higher if a reader buys directly from your site. But you'll probably lose more sales to people who just aren't comfortable buying from a stranger, or prefer buying at a retailer where they already have an account or perhaps can combine their shipments.

Selection is important to book buyers, so the best strategy for authors and publishers is to be visible everywhere and available through every possible retail channel. "You need to be channel-agnostic," says Bill Schubart, president of Resolution Inc., a consulting firm. "All of the power has moved from you, the publisher, to your customer, the readers. They will buy the book how, when and where they want. Your job is to make it easy and intuitive."

• **Static Web sites.** Repeat exposure encourages sales, so your Web site must encourage repeat visits. Good static content can draw lots of traffic, but probably won't produce many book sales unless visitors return and are exposed to the book again. An easy way to add fresh content is by using a blog.

• **Offering no sample content.** Authorship and publishing is all about spreading your ideas. If you have a good book, your best advertising is your own writing. Offer your first chapter, table of contents, and index in a free PDF that visitors can download from your site.

# Selling on Amazon, beyond

Self-publishing authors whose titles aren't distributed through a trade publisher have three basic options for ensuring their books are available on Amazon:

- Print on demand
- Amazon Advantage
- Amazon Marketplace

## Print on demand

If your book is handled by a printer such as Lightning Source, it will automatically be available through Amazon and BarnesAndNoble.com. Also, Lightning Source titles are available through Ingram Book Co. and Baker & Taylor, the two primary U.S. book wholesalers.

For more information about print on demand, consult the Recommended Reading section of this book.

## Amazon Advantage

Amazon Advantage is the company's inventory consignment program for small and midsize publishers.

With Advantage, publishers ship books to Amazon, which warehouses them and lists them for sale on the Web site. Amazon handles the orders, customer service, and shipping. Advantage members pay an annual fee of $29.99 and provide a 55 percent wholesale discount. In other words, if the full retail price of your book is $20, you'll receive $9 for each copy sold. For your previous month's sales, Amazon will deposit money into your checking account via electronic funds transfer.

Advantage has two major incentives for publishers:

- It provides your book with the same exposure as titles from other publishers having wide distribution and big marketing budgets.

- Amazon shows your title as available for "one-day shipping," which boosts sales.

You can apply online for the Advantage Program and submit your title for consideration. If approved, you'll list your book in Amazon's catalog, provide descriptive content, and ship books to an Amazon warehouse. When customers purchase your title, Amazon processes the order within 24 hours. Amazon tracks your inventory and sends e-mail requests for more copies according to customer demand.

If your title is enrolled in Advantage, it will also appear for sale on other Web sites such as Borders.com, Target.com, VirginMega.com and Waldenbooks.com.

Publishers must retain North American distribution rights to participate in Advantage, and your book must have a scannable barcode and valid ISBN.

## Amazon Marketplace

Most publishers use a distributor to get books into the hands of retailers. Some small publishers and self-publishing authors prefer to handle sales fulfillment themselves, for a variety of reasons. Handling the shipping provides access to buyer information, giving publishers who sell a line of related books the ability to upsell and pitch new titles directly to those buyers. When bookstores or Amazon handle sales, the publisher doesn't know who's buying the books.

Anyone with a U.S. bank account can open an Amazon seller account to list copies of books for sale. One advantage of Marketplace is that Amazon handles payment collection. Funds are deposited to your bank account in about a week, and sellers receive a shipping credit to help cover shipping costs.

Sellers pay Amazon a 15 percent commission on Marketplace sales and miscellaneous fees of $1.23 and 99 cents per transaction. The 99-cent fee on each sale is waived, however, if you become an Amazon Pro-Merchant subscriber. If you sell more than 40 books per month, the subscription pays for itself. Having a Pro-Merchant subscription also provides access to bulk listing and inventory tools that can help automate your bookkeeping.

## Catalog accuracy

Like Woody Allen once remarked about life, 80 percent of book sales success is "just showing up." The more information potential buyers know about your book, the more likely they are to buy it. Your book's detail page on Amazon is where readers make their buying decision. The address is:

**www.Amazon.com/gp/product/ISBN**

Replace the above letters ISBN with your book's ISBN digits.

Ensure your book's cover art is displayed on your book's Amazon product page. Despite the popular saying to the contrary, people *do* judge a book by its cover. It's amazing how many books on Amazon lack a cover image, something easily corrected by the publisher. Perception is everything: Shoppers who notice a missing cover image might assume the book isn't available. In a study of 20,000 titles where a missing cover image was replaced, sales rose an average of 60 percent, according to BarnesAndNoble.com.

Ensure your title's bibliographic data is displayed properly on Amazon at least once a week, including title, description, editorial reviews, format, number of pages, and other basic data. Most book sales occur on Amazon after a customer searches for keywords related to a book, so if any of this information isn't displayed correctly, readers can't find your book.

The fastest method for correcting a listing is to use the catalog update form on Amazon's site. At the bottom of the book's detail page, find the blue suggestion box labeled **Feedback**, and click Update product info. Here you can submit corrections using Amazon's Catalog Update Form for these elements:

- Title
- Author
- Publisher
- Binding

- Number of pages
- Publication date
- Edition
- Volume
- Format
- Language

Add or change descriptive content to your book's detail page here:

**www.Amazon.com/publishers**

Click the link for Submit correct requests and then Online content form. After providing your contact information and your book's ISBN, you'll see boxes where you can insert your book's description, author information, reviews, and more. The new material should appear on your book's product page within about five business days.

## Handling sales on your site

Offering your book for sale directly on your Web site can provide the highest profit margin. For those who sell downloadable books from their own site, the sale price is nearly all profit, excepting credit-card fees.

But many authors who sell directly on their Web site also offer a range of other options, like buying links to Amazon or Barnes & Noble. Some people are just more comfortable buying from a familiar merchant like Amazon. Authors who want to encourage sales through their own Web site can do so by offering something a bit extra, such as signed books or free shipping only for direct sales.

## Google Checkout

PayPal has been a popular tool among Internet merchants for years, but in 2006 Google launched its own payment service, Google Checkout.

Checkout has the potential for revolutionizing sales of books and other items over the Internet, since purchases can be made from any participating vendor using a single Google login. Google Checkout payments are fairly easy to add to any Web site or blog, using cut-and-paste code. Google Checkout also works with Google's search advertising program, AdWords, giving advertisers an easy solution for attracting customers and processing the resulting sales.

Google Checkout could also undermine one of Amazon's key advantages—checkout convenience. For more information, see:

**www.Checkout.Google.com**

# Other major online retailers

Barnes & Noble is the biggest U.S. multi-channel bookseller, the leading brick-and-mortar bookseller, and No. 2 to Amazon in online sales. "More and more people are researching online before they go into stores to buy," said Kate Zeman, director of trade book merchandising at BarnesAndNoble.com. "That's something we're seeing—what we're doing on our Web site influences sales in our stores."

## Barnes & Noble

Barnes & Noble's key device to promote cross-channel sales is its loyalty card program. Members pay $25 annually and receive a 10 percent discount online and in stores, in additional to several special offers during the year.

BarnesAndNoble.com also features author interviews and online courses. Perhaps due to its lower online sales volume relative to Amazon, BarnesAndNoble.com has much less user-generated content like reader book reviews.

Titles stocked in Barnes & Noble's warehouse are available for 24-hour delivery, but those supplied by wholesalers show as "usually ships in 2 to 3 days." If your book is available through a national wholesaler such as Ingram or Baker & Taylor, it will be available for order on BarnesAndNoble.com.

## BookSense

**www.BookSense.com** gives independent bookstores a way to have an Internet shopping site without making big technology investments. It's the e-commerce arm of the American Booksellers Association's BookSense program.

BookSense uses the wholesaler Ingram Book's iPage database to provide book listings for its 475 participating stores. Fulfillment is handled by the store or Ingram.

If your book is available through Ingram, it should be available on participating BookSense store sites, said Mark Nichols, BookSense director of marketing.

For books not available through Ingram, publishers can add a title to BookSense's database as long as it has a valid ISBN. Send your title, ISBN, author, publisher, bibliographic data, and cover art to **AddaBook@Booksense.com**.

Paid placement is also available through BookSense, which operates a co-op reimbursement program to help its members defray the costs of Web sites. BookSense handles the paperwork of aggregating offers from publishers who want to have their titles featured on BookSense sites for at least one month. Stores who accept the co-op offer must order at least five copies of the promoted title, unless the publisher specifies a higher minimum.

The co-op program provides for face-out display of physical copies of the book in the store, display on the store's Web site, and sales reporting.

A different BookSense program enables publishers to get reading copies of their books into the hands of local independent booksellers through its "Advanced Access Program." Several times a month, BookSense e-mails more than 1,000 booksellers, listing advance readers or finished books offered for review by publishers.

Booksellers who see your review copy have the option of carrying your title and nominating it for the BookSense "Picks" list of recommended books.

Advanced Access participants can expect to receive e-mails from 25 to 50 booksellers who want to review your book. No specific results are guaranteed from the program, but it is a tool for publicizing your title to people who can provide word-of-mouth advertising in their communities. To enroll, send an e-mail to Peter Reynolds at **peter@booksense.com**. Indicate the title, author, publisher, ISBN, subject category, publication date, and the number of free copies you have to offer. Include a two-sentence book description and an e-mail address where booksellers can request their review copy.

Include all your enrollment information in one paragraph that can be easily inserted in a larger message to bookstores. Here's an example:

***************************

TITLE ABC by John Doe, (Publisher XXX, ISBN: 0-000-00000-0, $19.95, hardcover, September 2007, Mystery/Thriller). A two-sentence description goes here, maximum 50 words. XX number of Advance Reading Copies available.

mailto:yournamehere@emailaddress.com
***************************

Don't include Web site information, press releases, or cover art. It can take two to three weeks from the time you send your message until booksellers see it.

BookSense charges $100 per title, with discounts available for members of the Publishers Marketing Association. You can send a check payable to American Booksellers Association at: ABA, 200 White Plains Road, Tarrytown, NY 10591 ATTN: Sadie Evans. For information on how to pay with a credit card, send an e-mail to **sadie@bookweb.org**.

When you send review copies to BookSense members, enclose a thank you note and a reminder to "e-mail or write Dan Cullen **(Dan@Booksense.com)** if you like it."

More information about BookSense is available by sending an e-mail to **Staff@Booksense.com**.

# Ethics of online marketing

Perhaps nothing is more important to authors and publishers than their reputation. While it's perfectly fine to promote your work energetically, consider the way your promotion might appear to others. Sometimes there's a fine line between being aggressive and being overzealous.

In some cases, the boundaries are clear. For example, the CAN-SPAM Act outlawed unsolicited commercial e-mail, so it's inappropriate to market your book by sending e-mails to strangers. In other cases, you'll need to use your judgment. For example, one section of this book discusses how to persuade people to review your book on Amazon. But don't ask people who haven't read your book. And don't review your book yourself. Don't buy thousands of copies of your own book in a ploy to push it onto the bestseller list.

On the Internet, it's fairly easy to hide your identity, but often it comes back to haunt people who use it as a marketing technique.

## Shill reviews

For years it was rumored that several authors and publicists had posted flattering reviews of their own books on Amazon, anonymously. This dishonest tactic of writing shill reviews, sometimes called "astro-turfing," depends on contrived reviews to simulate a grass-roots movement for a book on Amazon.

Then in 2004, a computer glitch revealed it was true—the real names of the authors were displayed, earning them a lifetime of embarrassment. One was John Rechy, author of the bestselling novel *City of Night*. The ironic thing was that Rechy was a successful writer whose honors included a PEN-USA West lifetime achievement award. He wasn't famous, but he didn't need shill book reviews either. But that computer glitch made him much better known, though probably not in the way he'd hoped.

One medical doctor who has a book for sale on Amazon has submitted hundreds of reviews of other books, which serve primarily to point attention to his own book. Apparently the doctor isn't concerned that his reputation as an author has been tarnished, as he's continued the activity.

In response to years of controversy about abuse of its review system, in 2006 Amazon began requiring that reviewers have an account with a registered credit card before reviews can be submitted. The safeguard prevents individuals from using multiple accounts to submit phony reviews. However, customers aren't required to purchase a copy of a book from Amazon before reviewing it.

## Spam

This book is intended to encourage authors to promote their book energetically and ethically. However, on the Internet, remember that tactics that may seem perfectly fine to you could offend someone else. For example, in 2005 an author sent a series of e-mails announcing his book to a list of addresses harvested from Amazon's Web site. Several recipients were angry enough to post critical reviews of the book and lambast the author for "spamming." The headline of the book's top Spotlight Review declares, "this author is a spammer." It's not something that will favorably impress potential readers.

Many book-marketing consultants advise authors to enter articles about themselves and their book in Wikipedia.org, the popular online encyclopedia. However, the site's guidelines clearly state that Wikipedia is not to be used for personal promotion or to popularize products or Web sites. Articles that are deemed self-promotional are deleted. Likewise, many books are promoted on Craigslist.com, an online classified service operated by eBay, in apparent violation of the site's terms of service.

Plug your book relentlessly. But don't do something in the heat of the moment that could damage your credibility. The biggest asset authors and publishers have is their credibility with the public.

# About the author

Steve Weber is a former newspaper reporter and veteran of the U.S. Air Force. Since 2000, he has been an online book dealer, specializing in scarce scientific and mathematics books, as well as collectible fiction. He has been one of the most successful and highly rated booksellers on the major networks such as Amazon Marketplace and eBay.

In 2005, Weber wrote and published *The Home-Based Bookstore.* He generates awareness of the book by coaching novice and experienced book dealers on his bookselling blog:

**www.weberbooks.com/selling/selling.htm**

Weber holds a bachelor of science degree from the Perley Isaac Reed School of Journalism at West Virginia University. He is a member of the Publishers Marketing Association and the International Association of Online Communicators. A native of Charleston, W.Va., he resides in the Virginia suburbs of Washington, D.C., with his wife and their young daughter. Write to him at:

**Feedback@WeberBooks.com**

For additional information on book promotion, online publicity, and free updates for this book, see:

www.PlugYourBook.com

# Recommended reading

*Aiming at Amazon: The NEW Business of Self Publishing, or A Successful Self Publisher's System for Profiting from Nonfiction Books with Print on Demand and Book Marketing on Amazon.com* by Shepard. 2006. ISBN 093849743X.

*The Savvy Author's Guide to Book Publicity* by Warren. 2004. ISBN 0786712759.

*Publicize Your Book!: An Insider's Guide to Getting Your Book the Attention it Deserves* by Deval. 2003. ISBN 0399528636.

*Buzz Marketing with Blogs for Dummies* by Gardner. 2005. ISBN 076458457X.

*Publicity on the Internet* by O'Keefe. 1997, 2007.

*Print-on-Demand Book Publishing: A New Approach to Printing and Marketing Books for Publishers and Authors* by Rosenthal. 2004. ISBN 0972380132.

*1001 Ways to Market Your Books: For Authors and Publishers* by Kremer. 2006. ISBN 091241149X.

*Growing Your Business with Google, (The Complete Idiot's Guide to)* by Taylor. 2005. ISBN 1592573967.

*How to Publish and Promote Online* by Rose and Adair-Hoy. 2001. ISBN 0312271913.

*Guerrilla Marketing for Writers: 100 Weapons to Help You Sell Your Work* by Levinson, Frishman, Larsen. 2000. ISBN 089879983X.

# Index


AbeBooks.com, 115
AdSense, 169
Ad-Supported Access (Google), 145
Advanced Access Program (BookSense), 186
advertising, Web sites, 167
AdWords, 144, 171
affiliate partnerships, 174
affiliate programs, 167
Alexa.com, 89
*Alphabet of Manliness*, 82
Also-Bought list, 23, 36
amateur book reviews, 39
Amazon Advantage, 181
Amazon Associates, 167
Amazon Bestseller Campaigns, 31
Amazon Connect blogs, 122
Amazon digital audio, 149
Amazon Interesting People, 133
Amazon Marketplace, 182
Amazon Media Library, 113, 147
Amazon Pages, 149
Amazon profiles, 131
Amazon Sales Rank, 28, 33, 173
Amazon Shorts, 151
Amazon Standard Identification Number (ASIN), 125
Amazon tags, 112
Amazon Upgrade, 147
Amazon.com, 19
America Online, 164
American Booksellers Association, 185
Anderson, Chris, 21, 81
Appelbaum, Judith, 12
article banks, 156
ASINs, 125
Atom feed, 76
Audacity.Sourceforge.net, 62
Author Marketing Experts Inc., 96
author platforms, 81
AuthorsOnTheWeb.com, 54
AuthorViews, 12, 60

Baldacci, David, 58
Barnes & Noble, 185
Best Value (Amazon), 119
bestseller lists, 31
Bete, Tim, 83
Better Together (Amazon), 121
Bezos, Jeff, 24, 47, 127
bibliographic data, 183
Bird, Julie, 10
blog artwork, 76
blog categories, 74
blog comments, 70
blog design, 71
blog linking, 76
blog post, types of, 73
blog searching, 68
blog titles, 73
blog tour pitches, 93
blog tours, 87
blog traffic, 89
blog writing, 73

blog, MySpace, 105
Blogbasedbooks.com, 86
BlogBurst, 158
Blogger.com, 54, 69, 78
Bloglines.com, 69
blogs, 65
blog-to-e-mail service, 79
blooks, 85
Blurb.com, 86
book excerpts, 90
book recommendations, 19, 21, 24, 35
book recommendations, adjusting, 133
book recommendations, effectiveness of, 26
book reviews, writing, 129
book tags, 111
Booklist, 50
BookSense, 185
BookShorts.com, 60
BookSurge, 131
BookWire, 52
BookWrapCentral.com, 60
Branley, Bill, 84
bulletins, MySpace, 102
BusinessWire.com, 160
Buy X Get Y (BXGY), 119
Buzzell, Colby, 84
BXGY (Buy X, Get Y), 119

CAN-SPAM Act, 189
categories, Amazon, 25
ClickBank.com, 153
comment moderation, 71
comments, blog, 70
comments, MySpace, 101
Commission Junction, 169
content management, 66
copyright violations, 161
Corn, Jane, 10, 44
Cox, Jim, 52
critics, professional, 39
Customer Discussions (Amazon), 131
customer reviews, Amazon, 46

del.icio.us, 138
Dent, Harry S., 152
Dermansky, Marcy, 103
Deval, Jacqueline, 33
Digg.com, 141
digital content, 143, 151
Discoverspaces.live.com, 78
Doctorow, Cory, 56
Donohue, Keith, 39
Dubelman, Liz, 60
duplicate content penalty, 157
Dynamics of Viral Marketing, The, 26, 28

eBay, 164
eBay affiliate program, 169
eBay Stores, 166
e-books, 148, 151
Edelman, David Louis, 57
*Effect of Word of Mouth on Sales*
*Online Book Reviews*, 47
*Elder Staves*, 97
electronic books, 148, 151
e-mail marketing, 33, 78, 189
e-mail subscriptions, 78
eMediaWire.com, 160

eReleases.com, 160
Evslin, Tom, 85
expert status, 155
EzineArticles.com, 156

Facebook, 98
FeedBlitz.com, 79
Feedburner.com, 79, 158
Feedster.com, 68
*Fifty two Projects Random Acts of Everyday Creativity*, 83
Flickr.com, 84, 111
folksonomies, 111
Foreword Magazine, 52
Freakonomics.com, 56
Fresh Books, 122
Friends, Amazon, 43, 132
Friends, MySpace, 100
Friendster, 98

GarageBand, 62
GoArticles.com, 157
GoDaddy.com, 53
Godin, Seth, 57, 63, 71
Google Alerts, 73
Google Analytics, 176
Google Book Search, 143
Google Checkout, 153, 184
Google Customized Search, 140
Google Groups, 163
Google Library, 145
Google News, 159
Google PageRank, 89
Google Pages, 54
Google Print on Demand, 146
Google Sandbox effect, 179
Greeley, Greg, 21
Greenwald, Glenn, 83
guest blogging, 87

Hackoff.com, 85
Herman, Jeff, 12
HipCast.com, 62
Holland Rogers, Bruce, 151
Hollows, Phil, 79
*Home-Based Bookstore, The*, 192
*How Would a Patriot Act?*, 83
HP Labs, 26
Huenefeld, John, 12

*I'm Not the New Me*, 84
IceRocket.com, 69
IdeaMarketers.com, 157
iMovie, 61
Instant Online Access (Google), 145
International Association of Online Communicators, 13
*Into Thin Air*, 19
iPod, 61
iTunes, 61

*Julie and Julia*, 65

keyword density, 70, 177
Kilmer-Purcell, Josh, 100
Kirkus Discoveries, 52
Kirkus Reports, 52
Kirkus Reviews, 50
Klausner, Harriet, 43
Krakauer, Jon, 19
Kremer, John, 12

Laimo, Michael, 99
Library Journal, 50
Library of Congress, 112
LibraryThing, 114
Librivox.org, 62
Listible.com, 142
Listmania, 123
LiveJournal.com, 54
*Long Tail, The*, 21, 81

Maddox, 82
McClure, Wendy, 84
McCullough, David, 151
media publicity, 158
MetricsMarket.com, 89
Midwest Book Review, 51
Miranda, Elisha, 109
Mobipocket, 148
Montano, Christine McNeil, 10
Movie Maker, 61
multimedia, 59
Murillo, Kathy Cano, 109
*My War*
    *Killing Time in Iraq*, 84
MyBlogLog.com, 176
MySpace, 97
MySpace blogs, 104
MySpace groups, 105
MySpace.com, 54

negative reviews, 47
netscape.com, 142
NetworkSolutions.com, 55
New York Times Best Sellers, 32

O'Keefe, Steve, 1, 10, 87
Oliverez, Steven, 97
Omakase, Amazon, 168
Orkut, 98
Ouzounian, George, 82

Pacelli, Lonnie, 152
PageRank, Google, 90, 137
paid placement, 119
Patron Saint Productions, 96
Payloadz.com, 153
PayPal, 153
pay-per-click advertising, 171
personalization, 23
pinging, blog, 76
podcasting, 61
PodioCast, 62
Porco, Linda, 39
Poundy.com, 84
Powell, Julie, 65
Poynter, Dan, 12, 52
press releases, 159
press rooms, 58
pricing, discounting, 135
print on demand, 146, 181
PRLeads.com, 158
PRLeap.com, 160
PRNewswire.com, 160
ProductWikis (Amazon), 130
PRWeb.com, 160
*Publicize Your Book*, 33

queer fiction, 112
Quick, William, 85

reader involvement, blogs, 88
Really Simple Syndication, 157
Rechy, John, 189

Register.com, 54
reputation, 155
reviews, 39
reviews, fee-based, 51
reviews, negative, 47
reviews, shill, 189
reviews, Spotlight (Amazon), 47
reviews, trade, 50
Rollyo.com, 140
Rosenthal, Morris, 10, 22, 85
RSS, 157
RSS feeds, 76, 115

sample content, 156
Sansevieri, Penny, 96
Scottoline, Lisa, 56
search engine optimization, 177
Search Inside the Book (Amazon), 126
Search Suggestions (Amazon), 140
Send2Press.com, 160
Shepard, Aaron, 10, 57
ShortShortShort.com, 152
Simpson, Joe, 19
Single New Product e-mails (Amazon), 121
SiteMeter.com, 176
So You'd Like to... guides, 125
social bookmarking, 138
social networking, 109
social search, 137
Spalding, Tim, 114
spam, 189
spam comments, 70
Spotlight Reviews, Amazon, 46
StatCounter.com, 176
Statistically Improbable Phrases (Amazon), 128
steampunk, 112
Swickis, 139
syndication, content, 155

tag-based marketing, 115
tagging, 138
tagging, books, 111
tags, Amazon, 112
tags, problems with, 116
tags, recommendations from, 113
Talese, Nan, 39
taxonomies, 111
Taylor, Dave, 14, 178
TeachingBooks.net, 60
Technorati.com, 68, 88
Tell a Friend feature (Amazon), 125
*The Stolen Child*, 39
Thompson, Clive, 69
TitleZ.com, 174
Top 8, MySpace, 103
Top Reviewers, Amazon, 41
*Touching the Void*, 19
trackbacks, 75
traffic reports, 176
trailers, book, 59
Tribe.net, 98
*Twins*, 103
TypePad.com, 78

Usenet, 163

vertical search, 139
videos, book, 59

VidLit.com, 59
viral marketing, 59
virtual author tours, 87

Wagner, Matt, 122
Web logs, 65
Web sites, 53
Weber Books, 4, 192
Weber, Steve, 192
Wheaton, Wil, 83
*Why Authors Are Cranky*, 151
Wikert, Joe, 86
wikis, 130
Windows Live Book Search, 146
wisdom of crowds, 138
Woods, Stuart, 152
word of mouth, 35
word verification, 71
WordPress, 56

Yahoo Groups, 164
Yahoo News, 159
Yahoo Podcasts, 62
Yahoo Search Marketing, 172
Yamaguchi, Jeff, 83
*Yiddish with Dick and Jane*, 59
YouTube.com, 59, 142

Zeman, Kate, 185